THE REAL MAN'S COOKBOOK

How, When, What and Why to Cook

W. J. RAYMENT

HATS
OFF™

Published by Hats Off Books™
610 East Delano Street, Suite 104
Tucson, Arizona 85705 U.S.A.
www.hatsoffbooks.com

ISBN: 1-58736-009-8
LCCN: 00-108278

Cover design by Chad M. Bush
Book design by Atilla L. Vékony

Printed in the United States of America

For Robin,
a real man's understanding wife

TABLE OF CONTENTS

PASTA AND STARCHES   127

DESSERTS   143

INTRODUCTION

The obvious question on the reader's mind must be, "Why another cookbook?" The answer is simple. Most cookbooks are written for women and, for that reason, do not account for the delicate tastes and abilities that make up the part and parcel of a man. With the exception of barbecue, the domestic culinary arts have been closed to the typical American male.

The cookbook industry fairly screams out for a cookbook that can concisely and understandably meet the needs of average men. Many men, in these trying times of feminism, are forced to fend for themselves, or, as in my case, fend for their families. Or it may be that a fellow just wants to get his greasy hands on a ripe tomato and a flank steak.

Being the cook of the house, I also feel an urgent need to lay to rest notions of cooking as a pansy sport. In manly circles, it is thought of in the same light as badminton or croquette, fit only for the effeminate. In reality, cooking is more akin to the rough-and-tumble sport of baseball, borrowing such terms as batter and fowl. It also requires plates and heavy mitts for effective play. Its participants need, in equal parts, power, finesse and intelligence.

Beyond sports analogies, cooking also demands the use of a vast array of tools easily as specialized as auto-mechanics or electronics. A cook may use spatulas, rolling pins and calendars. Hammers and a variety of knives come in handy, too. Not that the art of cooking is so complex that you need to take a battery of courses at the local vocational technical college to do it. Cooking is only as complex as you wish to make it. You can make a simple bowl of oatmeal in the microwave or a complex Chicken Cordon Bleu. You can whip up a bowl of canned soup or make baklava from "scratch."

I suppose I should pause here to explain the word "scratch" so that the reader does not presume I am falling back on my baseball analogy. For a cook to make something from scratch is to attempt to throw together a palatable dish using only basic ingredients. When I say "basic," I mean basic. These ingredients are the elements that form the chemical chart we were all forced to memorize in chemistry class in high school. I'm not big on scratch recipes. So to use this cookbook, you will not be required to break out your son's chemistry set. Luckily, in the modern world, most carbon-based consumables have already been formulated into a readily edible substance. For example, you don't need to go through the trouble of making pie crust from flour, water and polyunsaturated gelatinized sunflower seed oil. You can get it from a box, roll it out and flop it in a tin. Or you can even buy the crust pre-made. Heck, you can just buy the whole pie frozen.

This prompts a second question, and a good question: "If I can get food pre-made, for example in a restaurant, then why bother cooking at all?"

I have racked my brain and scrounged up several good reasons. First, any real man is as much of a tight wad as I am. He can't afford to go out to dinner every night and going out on a date makes this procedure doubly expensive.

An even better reason is that no one makes food to my taste as well as I do. I know just how much paprika and hot sauce to dump into my chili and how many onions to toss into a chicken teriyaki. I know enough to keep my food simple, and to avoid the baser elements on chemical chart: no molybdenum, ferrous oxide, Tang instant breakfast mix or Brussels sprouts.

The best reason to cook is for the sheer joy of it. There are many who would argue with me about this. Even my own mother tells me what a drag cooking can be. But cooking is like any other activity. You get out of it in proportion to what you put into it (and this has nothing to do with Newton's Law of Conservation of Matter and Energy that we were also forced to memorize in high school). I get a bang out of cooking because I make it fun, and I make the food I like. When a dish turns out to taste good there is also the satisfaction derived from a job well done.

Finally, if it has been too long since your wife or girlfriend granted you her favors, cooking works wonders where the usual pleading and begging will fail. You can pretend to be the sensitive lover, when all you have done is throw a can of mushroom soup over a slab of beef and dumped some instant mashed potatoes into a pan of boiling water.

This book is designed to show the average male what to cook, how to cook it (and like it). It is jam-packed with all kinds of tips and recipes that have stood me in good stead for years, stuff that tastes good, stuff that looks good and even stuff that women will like.

Have fun and eat hearty!

ABOUT COOKING

How to Cook in General

Women are the touchiest of creatures. Their pride is as fragile as a flower. I severely wounded a woman once by stating categorically and emphatically that a certain dish was better even than sex. After she slapped me crosswise with an open handed roundhouse, I was forced to explain to her that my statement was a mere euphemism, a figure of speech, rhetoric. Though I begged forgiveness for several weeks, I was, from then until the end of our relationship, forced to live a life of undiluted abstinence.

The truth of the matter remains: the dish held for me, at that moment, a greater attraction and intense sensual pleasure than anything I had theretofore experienced. I had only made the mistake of expressing this thought aloud. I have subsequently learned that pleasures of the senses are tied to the moment and it seems that the latest pleasure of any intensity is the best . . . ever.

An Epicurean is someone whose life is geared toward always seeking pleasure. I do not necessarily advocate this approach to life. If anything, I tend towards the stoical, but there is something to be said for eating a good meal on occasion, and it can be made even better by mixing it with other pleasures such as ESPN or a competitive game of eight ball on the pool table in the basement.

Unfortunately, there is not always someone around to do the cooking and to allow you to live in the manner to which you would like to become accustomed. Sometimes there is no one who can do the job as well as you can. You may find that your wife or girlfriend does not cook as well as she would like to think. It is at times like these that you will want to pick up the holy spatula and perform a few culinary miracles. The only problem is that you do not want to offend your spouse in the process. I suggest a tactful appeal to her better nature. Tell her that there is a sale on negligee at JCPenney. If she rushes off to the store, then you are set for the evening. You can whip up your favorite meal in her absence, and when she returns, enjoy the fruits of your labor. If she doesn't rush off immediately go to Plan B and tell her you have a recipe that is even better than sex. She is sure to leave you alone long enough for you to do some serious cooking.

The Oven As a Time-Saver

In preparing a meal, the one thing you do not want to do is take all day about it. Cooking can be an enjoyable experience, but there are sure to be other activities in which you also wish to engage. You will learn time conservation from this cookbook. How you use the time saved is entirely up to you. You can run your

Mercury outboard in a trash can full of water, or oil all of those electrical tools that hang from a peg board in the garage.

One of the greatest time-savers in cooking is the oven. Don't be fooled by those who tell you that a microwave is the fastest way to cook. Sure, a dish gets done faster, but you have to get up from your Tom Clancy novel every five minutes or so just to stir something or turn something or add something or uncover something. More time is spent in total aggravation than Clancy spends describing the inner-workings of a nuclear sub. Although stuff put in the oven often takes longer to cook, it saves you time by allowing you to ignore the dish. An oven will cook evenly and thoroughly without you having to attend to a beeper every few seconds.

You will undoubtedly notice that most recipes that require oven-time call for 375°F. In most cases this is just a number. The fact is that many dishes may be cooked faster or slower depending on your preferences. Meats can be cooked as high as 425° and still have the inside get done before the outside is burnt. Most things can also be cooked more slowly in the oven, this will allow you to time dishes so that everything you have decided on for a meal gets done at the same time.

Knowing how long it takes for stuff to get done is important. There is a general rule of thumb. Most plain vegetables take about five minutes (in the microwave), starches take fifteen to twenty minutes (on the stove top) and meats usually take forty-five minutes or more (in the oven). This means that you should always work backward. That is, start the meat first, then the starch, then the vegetable.

Tools of the Trade

Just as in woodworking, there are a near infinite number of tools you can purchase to make your life easier and your work more precise. Also, like woodworking, these tools are not all strictly necessary. A tall smooth water glass can substitute for a rolling pin just as a screwdriver and a hammer can, on occasion, substitute for a drill. The average tea cup holds exactly eight ounces, and can be substituted for a marked measuring cup.

Yet there are items that you are certain to need. A pan, fork and spoon are all handy items. A spatula is also a good thing to have and not just for spanking wayward children. Aluminum foil is useful for a variety of applications. Probably the most important tool in cooking is the knife. I am not talking about your regular old namby-pamby butter knife. You will need something sharp that will go easily through animal or vegetable matter. Knives are kind of the screwdrivers of the culinary technician's world. You can never have too many knives; they are useful for everything, and they get mislaid very easily.

The best investment you will ever make is a set of sharp knives. They come in a variety of forms from paring knives to big ol' butcher knives. I find the fiercer looking knives tend to be unwieldy and not useful for much other than cutting off tree limbs and carving an occasional turkey. Paring knives are best in accomplishing most tasks. You will find yourself cutting carrots, slicing pork and peeling potatoes.

There are power tools in cooking too. Nearly every repetitive task has been automated. There are mixers and blenders and slicers and dicers, can openers and popcorn makers. It is amazing how quickly you may peel an apple with an apple peeler, or grind up carrots with a juicer. Yet unlike a power drill, a kitchen appliance cannot necessarily be set aside and ignored until the next time it is needed. It must be CLEANED, and the consequences of not cleaning them can be disastrous. Anyone who has left the crud to dry at the bottom of a blender knows what I mean. No man that I have ever met enjoys meticulously wiping food particles from the underside of a blender blade. Unless you are making mass quantities of a particular item, the savings in time provided in food processing by an electric appliance may be far outweighed by the time spent in cleaning the apparatus.

Aprons and Other Protective Gear

There is a need in cooking for certain protective gear. In the introduction, I mentioned the ubiquitous oven mitt. Without it a person would not be able to handle hot baking dishes or make puppet gestures for the kids. A CO_2 canister is also handy to have nearby in case a load of French fries attempts a revolution.

Aprons are a delicate subject for most men. Some will wear them. Others will not. I must confess that an apron can be a handy item of cover if you want to keep catsup stains off your coveralls. However, a man must be careful about the apron he wears. I would not be caught dead in one that has any frills on it or accentuates my narrow waste. If I am going to wear an apron, I prefer one that is made of black rubber and could also be used for aluminum arc welding.

Baking vs. Cooking

Although many recipes in this book use the oven, not many can really be called baking recipes. Baking involves yeast, pastries and lots of flour floating like pollen in the air. Baking requires a tall hat with a puffy crown.

If there are few baking recipes here, it is because of the baking union's requirement of an exactness, of which I personally am incapable. Even a slight variation in a baking recipe results in a product that is likely to look as though it has been pulled from a kiln rather than an oven.

A cooking recipe, in most cases, can be adjusted, substituted and flipped upside down—the result will still be palatable. The difference is a function of the fact that baking is a chemistry experiment and cooking is an artistic endeavor.

Alcohol at Meal Time

I don't typically drink adult beverages at mealtimes. Nevertheless, on a Friday afternoon, after a long week of slaving over a hot stove—you know, "bring home the bacon and fry it up in a pan,"—I will succumb to a minor indulgence. Now, there are those of us who prefer wine and others of us who prefer beer. It is really no reflection on the degree of a person's manliness which way he leans. However, it is a reflection on the kind of manliness.

There is continental manliness, where one knows what wine to drink with what and when to do it and does it all with a panache that makes the ladies swoon. This kind of manliness certainly has its advantages and I do fake it whenever the situation calls. However, there is the other manliness under which most of us regular guys fall. We know enough to drink red wine with red meat and white with white meat, at least in most cases. Yet, more than this, we know that a good cold bottle of brew would taste better than either. Thus, throughout this book, for most main dishes I have recommended a particular brand of beer rather than a wine.

Don't worry if you can't find the brand mentioned, most others will readily supply the place. By the way, I reserve the hard liquor for when my wife decides to cook.

Universal Ingredients

There are some ingredients that will go into darn near anything. We all know about the basic spices like salt and pepper. Parsley is another of those spices that will add a positive flavor to any dish. My favorite universal ingredient is the carrot, not so much because Bugs Bunny popularized its consumption, but because it adds color and flavor to what otherwise might be some pretty drab dishes. Not that I am into aesthetics or care how stuff looks. As far as I am concerned, all my food could be as brown as mud. Heck, the browner the better. But if you have to please others (wife, kids or even company), it is sometimes best to humor their weaknesses.

If the carrot is the universal vegetable, then the raisin is the universal fruit. It can be tossed into near any sweet dish to make it just a bit more—well—fruity.

As you can imagine, the chicken is the universal meat. It can be substituted for any other meat, with the possible exception of liverwurst for which nothing is the best substitute. After a whiff of liverwurst you won't want to be eating anything anyway.

Preheating the Oven

What is it with all these recipes that specify "Preheat the oven to . . ."? As far as I can tell, preheating is just a big waste of electricity or gas or whatever it is that powers your oven. I believe that recipe writers throw it into their recipes for two reasons. First, they want to sound professional. Second, they want to impose uniformity upon the mass of humanity. Because ovens will likely have an uneven warm up rate, it is impossible for them to calculate how long a dish will have to stay in an oven if it is NOT preheated. They do not have enough confidence in the individual. I have even less confidence in the average cookbook writer, as their time for baking never coincides with reality. It is nearly always short.

You will note that I do have confidence in you. Nowhere will you find a notation insisting on "preheating." Rather, I will specify a time for baking and hope you will check on the dish then. If it is not done, check it periodically thereafter. Alternatively, you may use the following formula to calculate the time it takes for a dish to bake to finish: $a^2+b^2=c^2$. Where a is the temperature required; b is the time specified; and c is the square of the hypotenuse.

The Right Combinations

You need to know more than just what ingredients combine together to make a palatable dish; you need to know what dishes go together to make a good meal.

All kinds of theories have been bandied about by nutritionists, health scientists and dietitians. We have the four major food groups, the food pyramid and any number of cockamamie theories. Most of us can tell what constitutes a good meal without resorting to a textbook. And if you are in any doubt about trusting your own instincts and senses, you can use my simple method of color-coding.

We all know that food gets mixed up once it has been consumed and the result will inevitably be brown. My theory proposes that there is an optimum brownness that you should achieve, a burnt sienna or a plain Crayola brown. Knowing this to be true, you do not strictly want to serve a meal that has all light foods. For example: chicken breast, boiled potatoes, cottage cheese and corn. Sure, it's an okay meal, but something is lacking. You want to throw something green in there. Nearly any green vegetable will do. Alternatively, you don't want to eat just plain green vegetables. Not only will it not fill you up, it will have adverse effects upon the digestive system.

So, when you are putting together a meal, think of yourself as a painter. If you must, get out that old color wheel that you saved from art class in high school. Put together something that hits as many of the colors as possible on the spectrum. I only will caution you to go light on the blues, and if you need red, beets give you a big bang for the buck.

Meal Presentation

When you are dealing with women or other forms of company such as in-laws, there will be some need for gussying up whatever meal you have decided upon. In general, women like to eat foods that look neat and orderly. I know that when my wife fixes her plate she strictly avoids any mixing of foods. By the time I am done loading my plate, I may as well have made a casserole. This may mean setting the table and even placing a napkin beside the plate. It may mean going to the extreme of serving the vegetables and potatoes in a bowl.

If you are into this sort of thing, or are required by circumstance to indulge a relative or friend, there is one rule to remember: serve buffet style. If that proves impractical, the fork goes on the left with the napkin. The knife and spoon go on the right. Water glass is on the right. Bread dish on the left. And if you haven't yet run out of room, the plate goes in the middle of it all. The beer bottle, by the way, can be set on the floor next to your chair—back left leg. That way it is easy to grab when you lean back after wolfing down a plate of your own favorite dish.

I tend not to cook for many formal occasions. I have finally accustomed my wife to the idea that serving dishes are unnecessary and that food can be served directly from the pan. When my wife is not about I just eat out of the pan.

BEEF

Here's the Beef

After a hard day on the dusty range, the cowboy sits near the camp fire, his tin cup full of hot joe, with a plate of canned beans and . . . and what? It's not the leg of a roast squib in a tarragon sauce or a delicate crepe suzette. Indeed, there is only one thing that could possibly complete this meal. The cowboy has a thick slab of beef standing tall and rugged, like a rocky island among a sea of brown beans and molasses.

The image of cow and man is inseparable and the mystique extends even to our language. For example, to "beef up" is to make something stronger, better, and tougher. "Where's the beef?" is a rhetorical question in a search for substance. "Bull-headedness" is a term that embodies the best of the manly virtues.

Men are known to be fond of steaks, roasts, shoulders, ribs and just about anything that can be sliced, hacked or bitten from a cow, short of the hooves and the eyeballs. Simply, mention "prime rib" at an all male venue and you will see eyes stare longingly into space and mouths water.

This attraction between *man*kind and beefkind has been a hallmark of human history. It runs deep into our pastoral ancestry. Cattle were once the primary form of barter and a prime store of wealth. At that time, when someone got their "pound of flesh," it was a legitimate transaction.

A doctor of physiology would attribute man's inclination for beef to a biological need for protein. A Freudian psychologist might put it down as a subconscious desire to die before our wives by cholesterol poisoning. A behaviorist would explain it as an image thing. Indeed, there is some truth in all of these explanations. After all, beef cattle are the biggest, strongest, meanest, fattest, and most protein packed of creatures that we humans typically eat.

In the end, though, life just isn't that complicated. Beef simply tastes good. That's why we eat it. Try a beef recipe that defies philosophic argument: Beef Potpie.

Beef Potpie

Serving Size: 6
Preparation Time: 30 minutes
Ingredients:
1 pound hamburger
1 potato
1 carrot
1 onion
3 mushrooms—fresh
1 tablespoon parsley
1 teaspoon basil
1 pie crust
1 can mushroom soup
1 cup peas—frozen

Fry the hamburger in a frying pan. While this process is going on, cut up and toss into the frying pan all the vegetables and spices except the frozen peas. When hamburger is browned, drain off excess fat.

Add the mushroom soup to frying pan and thoroughly mix — dump contents into the pie crust. If you have extra pie dough, crisscross strips across the top of the pie, or you can also put a solid layer across the top.

Bake at 375° for an hour.

Serving Ideas: This is good with rice.

Picking out Meat and Looking for Marbling

It is typical in a cookbook to examine and expound upon the various cuts of meat. Some will even describe in detail how to butcher a beef cattle and from where to extract the most tender portions. However, this information is superfluous. In our age of modern convenience it is unlikely a person will be required to hand-carve a carcass hanging in his personal meat locker.

Rather, there are two easy rules to follow in picking out beef. First, if you are looking for a roast, get a thick hunk of beef. Second, if you are looking for a steak, get one that is skinnier. Of course it does get a bit more complicated if you are looking for a *good* steak. Obtaining the elusive *good* steak depends more on the thickness of your bankroll than the thickness of the meat.

You will find the more expensive cuts of steak have something called "marbling." Marbling is really just several thin striations of fat that run between the strands of muscle that make up the slab of meat. It is called marbling because it resembles red and white marble tile. The striations of fat break down when the steak is being cooked and keep the piece of meat tender. A lack of marbling will generally result in a tough steak. If it is any consolation, the tougher steak undoubtedly has less cholesterol.

When in doubt, you can always ask your friendly neighborhood butcher. Just be polite; this is a man who has many sharp knives and he knows how to use them.

Grilled Steak

Serving Size: 4
Preparation Time: 15 minutes
Ingredients:
2 pounds beef T-bone steak
1 dash salt
1 dash pepper
1 onion
1 tablespoon butter

On the grill, simply flop on the raw steak, sprinkle on the salt and pepper. Brown both sides and that's it. Fry the onions in a separate frying pan, per instructions below.

When the rain is pouring or it's too cold to stand around the grill with a beer and a fearsome looking two-pronged fork, try frying your steaks. Admittedly, you will not get the same charcoal flavor, yet an iron frying pan will impart a flavor all its own. Be sure to warm the skillet first. Place a slice of butter or margarine in the pan. When it is bubbling, spread it around the base of the pan, and throw in the meat. Add onions, salt and pepper. Brown each side for approximately five minutes . . . more or less depending on your taste. This is a good meal for a Sunday afternoon in the fall when your favorite football team is hashing it out with the Oakland Raiders. Don't forget to fry it fast to preserve the juices and the tenderness.

Serving Ideas: With corn on the cob and baked potatoes.

Suggested Beer: Bud.

Preparation

In cooking up a piece of beef, it is, of course, best to at least loosely adhere to a recipe. Yet there is a general guideline with regard to beef. *Cook steak as fast as you can and cook a roast as slow as you can.* As incongruous as these rules seem, they work.

A slow cooked steak will yield something akin to the soles of the army boots your great-grandfather wore in the trenches during the First World War. Whether on a grill or on the stove top, cook the steak on at least medium-high and heat it as thoroughly as possible without over-burning the outside.

A roast in the oven at 375° needs to cook at least for three hours; five is good and more is even better. The only reason to stop cooking a roast is because a lynch mob will likely be coming after you if you do not soon produce a meal. Of course, there must be a point at which a roast will dry out—I have never had the patience to find out when that point is.

Six-Hour Stew

Serving Size: 6
Preparation Time: 30 minutes
Cooking Time: 5 hours and 59 minutes
Ingredients:
1½ pounds beef round
6 potatoes
4 carrots
4 mushrooms—fresh
1 can stewed tomatoes
1 can green beans
¼ cup tapioca
1 dash pepper
1 tablespoon garlic powder
1 tablespoon parsley

Cut the beef into chunks. Toss them into a Dutch oven or some kind of covered baking dish. Add potatoes, carrots, sliced mushrooms. Dump cans of tomatoes and green beans over the top and then mix in the minute tapioca and spices. Cover; stick whole into the oven for five or six hours. Tastes great alone or can be served over bread.

Safe Handling

Meat should never be eaten raw—or even close to raw. Fire was invented for a very good reason—and it wasn't just so we could smoke a fine cigar after dinner. I'm not saying that you have to eliminate all trace of red in your meat. A little pink is okay. You just don't want to look like a sloppy vampire if a bit of au jus happens to dribble down your chin. And the effects later of an undercooked hunk of meat can be truly explosive.

You have heard it a million times before: Don't forget to wash your hands . . . before and after you handle meat, and like your mama told you, "USE SOAP!"

When to Cook Beef

We have established that beef is primarily a man's food. However, this doesn't mean that women cannot eat it too. Unfortunately for them, medical science has determined that chocolate is more in tune with their delicate taste buds. They cannot fully appreciate a blackened prime rib or a juicy T-bone. Yet they can enjoy it in a limited way. Thus it is appropriate to eat beef in the presence of the opposite sex — it's not quite like telling an off-color story — although the man should express some empathy for the woman's plight by offering to exchange her slab of New York Strip for a Hershey bar he just happens to have handy.

Summertime is classically steak time. Cooking outside is important to keep from overheating the house. Wintertime is great for roasts because having the oven on for several hours serves a dual purpose. Steaks seem to go with traditional summer food such as potato salad and cold beer. Roasts naturally require potatoes (cooked with the roast), carrots and mushrooms as well as the other traditional winter consumable — cold beer.

Beef is delicious any time. Hamburgers are good for outdoor barbecues when you have guests, and roasts are best when you want to fill the house for hours with a smell that reminds you of your grandpa's farm and your grandma, wearing her apron bending smilingly over a hot stove. It makes my nostrils twitch just thinking about it. For a great roast recipe try the one below, and once you've tried it straight, try it with half a bottle of beer tossed in for good measure.

Roast Beast

Serving Size: 6
Preparation Time: 30 minutes
Ingredients:
3 pounds beef
3 pounds potatoes
3 carrots
4 mushrooms
1 onion
3 teaspoons flour
2 tablespoons Worcestershire sauce
2 tablespoons honey

In a large Pyrex dish or ceramic roasting pan place all ingredients except flour. Be sure to clean and cut up the vegetables first. Add water to fill about a quarter of the dish. Cover tightly with tin foil or lid and pop into the oven at about 375°.

The longer you bake this, the tenderer the meat will be (up to a point anyway). When the roast has reached desired doneness (five hours, I find, is optimum, however, three will do fine), draw off ¾ of the juice and put in saucepan. Boil sauce.

While you are waiting for sauce to boil, mix flour with ¼ cup water. When sauce reaches boil, stir in flour mixture. Makes a fine lumpy gravy. When gravy is finished, remove roast and eat hardy.

Instead of all this work making the gravy, you might instead simply go with the juice or, alternatively, there is always the old reliable mushroom soup. If you use this last ingredient, simply pour it over the roast when you put it in the oven . . . you might want to leave off the honey in this case.

Vegetarianism and the Argument for Gravy

As you have undoubtedly gathered by this time, I am no vegetarian. Of all the vegetables, perhaps only spinach has the right to claim a manly attraction, but only because Popeye could convert it so readily into a show of strength.

The great allure of vegetarianism is a misplaced pacifism that seeks to extend human feeling to all animals. A calf's sad eyes as it watches its mother led to the slaughterhouse is truly a stark image. Yet if one sees life in terms of the natural order of the universe, we see that violent consumption is a fact of life for all creatures — that is either to consume or be consumed. I guess I prefer to be the consumer rather than the consumee.

The argument between us omnivores and the rag tag mass of vegetable eaters goes deeper yet, and has everything to do with gravy. A vegetarian can throw every good argument in the world at me regarding man's humanity to animals, man's greater health risks associated with eating animals or even reincarnation. One argument stops them all: gravy. You see, I eat vegetable matter too, especially the starches, like potatoes and rice. Without some kind of gravy or at least butter, these foods taste rather bland. Human life would be meaningless without gravy.

Finally, I know some vegetarians (the most fervent fanatics on the face of the earth when it comes to trying to convert others to their tasteless, drab existence). Some of these people could even be called my friends. The trouble they go through in order to achieve a semblance of protein in their diets is truly amazing. This leads me to believe that the human animal is not meant to be strictly vegetarian—just as he would die of scurvy if all he ate was meat.

Now that we have dispensed with the vegetarians and their arguments, it seems apropos to mention here that there are very few real men who are strictly vegetarian anyway.

Gravy

Serving Size: 10
Preparation Time: 10 minutes
Ingredients:
½ cup au jus
1 cup water
4 tablespoons flour
1 dash pepper
1 dash salt

In a saucepan, bring juice from meat and half of the water to a boil. Stir flour into the other half of the water until most of the lumps are gone—unless you like lumps in your gravy.

Add salt and pepper to boiling mixture. Then, while still stirring—this takes a bit of coordination but not as much as patting your head and rubbing your stomach at the same time—slowly pour in the flour and water mixture.

The gravy should thicken immediately. Let stand for at least thirty seconds or you will burn your lips.

Stroganoff

Serving Size: 4
Preparation Time: 30 minutes
Ingredients:
1 pound beef stew meat or hamburger
1 can cream of mushroom soup
8 ounces sour cream
1 onion
4 mushrooms
1 dash pepper
1 teaspoon oil
12 ounces egg noodles

This is a great, quick meal. Another of many that are made with the ubiquitous Campbell's mushroom soup.

Cut beef into strips. Fry in oil with sliced onions and mushrooms. When sufficiently brown, dump in the can of soup, and then dump in sour cream. Add pepper.

Boil egg noodles as per instructions on packet.

Lay down bed of noodles. Ladle on sauce.

Note: Don't call this dish "Strokinoff" in front of your guests. No one will want to eat it.

Suggested Beer: Heineken.

Serving Ideas: Serve with a green vegetable.

Poor Man's Meat

Meat loaf does not fit into any normal food category. I have listed it under beef merely for the sake of convenience. If we go by the name, the only item of food that it is sure to contain is meat. What kind of meat? It might be anything from the traditional hamburger to venison to lamb to pork to ground chicken to rabbit or any mixture thereof.

If the word "meat" is a nebulous description then the meaning of "loaf" could be even more variously interpreted. Typically a meat loaf may contain breadcrumbs, oatmeal, potato flakes or even sawdust (or something that tastes like sawdust). I do not recommend the latter ingredient as it is likely to cause splinters.

As for spices, vegetables, etc., well, the universe is a very large place. When you read the recipe, you realize that nearly any ingredient can be substituted or added as long as the basics are adhered to. That is, there must be meat and it must be in the form of a loaf.

Meat loaf has gathered an unfortunate reputation for being a poor man's entree. It is true that the ingredients of meat loaf are not exorbitantly priced. Yet, I find that the staples of a poor man's diet are often more to my taste and more healthy than foods patronized by the socially conscious.

Because of its variable nature, meat loaf can be made to anyone's taste. If you are partial to caviar and Calamatta olives then feel free to dump them into the mix. They will not only make the loaf more interesting, they will boost the relative cost of a dish to a realm more palatable to a person with expensive tastes. If you should attempt this though, it might be wise to change the name of the dish to something that sounds a bit more highbrow, for example, *pesce ouff bagguette*. Any name that sounds remotely French will be sure to impress friends and neighbors.

Like many other dishes that you will find in this book, meat loaf is great as a leftover. I am partial to meat loaf sandwiches, which is nothing more than a few thin slices of meat loaf between two pieces of bread with a little mustard to flavor it. No need to warm it. It is fine cold — better than most lunchmeats, in fact.

The following recipe is my standard form of meat loaf. Feel free to dress it up with your own favorite ingredients. As long as they are not ingredients typical to sweet dishes, you probably will find the result tasty. My mother likes to put chopped pickles in meat loaf. It is really quite good.

Meat Loaf

Serving Size: 8
Preparation Time: 30 minutes
Ingredients:
1 pound ground beef
1½ cups oatmeal—uncooked
1 onion—chopped
2 mushrooms—sliced
1 dash pepper—ground
1 dash garlic powder
1 tablespoon parsley
2 eggs
¼ teaspoon basil
1 dash dill weed
¼ cup catsup

This is another one of those hands-on dishes. Add all ingredients except catsup to a bowl and then squish them together with your bare hands. Don't use rubber gloves, as you do not get the full effect with them. Also, rubber gloves can impart a strange taste to your loaf. Shape the loaf to your desire in a deep cake pan of 9×13 or some similar dimension. This is a perfect dish for Valentine's Day, because it isn't too difficult to form a heart. It will be complete when you spread the catsup over the top as you would spread frosting on a cake.

Bake mixture at 375° for about 1½ hours.

Suggested Beer: Iron City Beer.

Serving Ideas: Good with instant mashed potatoes and corn.

Important Note: Do not serve to anyone who pretends to hold a Master's degree in any of the liberal arts. They are likely to look down on you for the rest of your life. You will forever be "provincial." Or better yet: do serve it to them and when you're done, tell them where you got the recipe.

Roast Steak

Serving Size: 4
Preparation Time: 15 minutes
Ingredients:
1½ pounds round steak
1 can Campbell's mushroom soup
6 carrots
1 dash pepper

This is kind of a hybrid between a steak and a roast and is one of my favorite recipes, if only because it is so easy to make.

In a baking pan, throw down the slab of meat. Peel and cut carrots into chunks. Scatter the carrots on the top of the meat. Dump can of soup over all. I always add a bit of pepper and you can put in some Worcestershire sauce too (but only if you can pronounce it).

Cover and bake for about 2½ hours, or until meat falls apart on your fork.

Serving Ideas: Serve with mashed potatoes and peas.

Suggested Beer: Red Wolf.

An Irish Reverie

Ireland is a wonderful place to visit. Admittedly the food there is not always particularly spicy. Nevertheless, it always seems to fill a gaping maw and fortify a flagging spirit. Ireland is one of the few countries that have successfully exported their atmospheres to little spots all over the United States. For the atmosphere of that land is not solely in the shamrocks, the ever-present rain or the friendly redheaded people. It's more an attitude that can be found in every Irish pub in America and every home that chooses to take up an Irish tune.

Thus it was no surprise to me on traveling through southern New Jersey to find a wee bit of the old country. I stopped in at an Irish pub and sidled up to the bar. On a TV hanging over the bar two pugs were boxing with all the skill and finesse of a couple of bulldogs. The barmaid's skirt ended well up her thighs and she had the good grace to keep them constantly within my view. Best of all, they had Guinness on tap. I thought I was in heaven. When I looked at the menu, I realized there was only one thing to order: Shepherd's Pie.

You've got to try the Shepherd's Pie recipe. At your discretion you can substitute either chicken breast or lamb for the hamburger.

Shepherd's Pie

Serving Size: 8
Preparation Time: 30 minutes
Ingredients:
1 pound hamburger
1 onion
1 carrot
1 cup peas
1 dash garlic powder
1 dash pepper
2/3 cup milk
4 tablespoons margarine
2 2/3 cups mashed potato flakes
1 can mushroom soup
2 slices cheddar cheese
3 dashes paprika

Fry hamburger, onion, carrot and peas in skillet, add garlic and pepper. Don't forget to drain the grease unless you have a cardiologist handy—full time.

Add mushroom soup to mixture and dump into bottom of some sort of baking pan.

Boil 2 2/3 cup water, milk and margarine in pan. When it comes to a boil—which doesn't take as long as you think, and if you let it boil over it can make a heck of a mess—remove from heat and add the potato flakes stirring vigorously until it becomes a paste-like gloppy substance . . . or at least it looks like your idea of mashed potatoes.

Spread this substance evenly over the hamburger mixture. Place slices of cheese on top and criss-cross the paprika. Cover the entire dish and put in the oven at 375° for ½ to 1 hour. Serve to shepherds or shepherdesses as the case may be.

Serving Ideas: This is one of those stand-alone dishes.

Recommended Beer: Guinness.

CHICKEN

You Are What You Eat

Chicken, like beef, conjures powerful images. Unfortunately for chickens, the representation is not a positive one. Most humans endeavor to avoid any association between themselves and the character of a chicken. Indeed, the mere mention of chickens brings to mind a frantic, frightened, unintelligent animal running in circles screaming at the top of its pitiful lungs. Personally, I hope that I would have a bit more dignity in expressing chagrin over the matter of the sky falling. Unlike Chicken Little, I would look up at the descending dome of the heavens and pronounce in a heavy Austrian accent, "Zee sky ist valling." Then I would shake my fist defiantly while running for cover, and shout, "I'll be BACK!"

One generally thinks of chickens as females. This is because most of the chickens that manage to live productive lives are females. Females are, after all, the only birds capable of egg production. It just so happens that in modern society, the males aren't good for much more than insemination and being eaten by us humans. This was not always the case. Roosters, at one time, had a much more prominent place in Chickendom. At that time, they earned for themselves an exemption from the timorous stereotype that is due to the activity of their sisters. They would fight at the drop of a hat, standing up to creatures many times their own size. Our language reflects this bravado; when a person is referred to as cocky, he is thought of as gutsy, if vain and arrogant. I suspect that if it were not for the interference of modern economies of scale, male dominance would be maintained in at least one of the animal species.

Somehow we humans have let the natural order erode for both chickens and mankind. Like hens, women have gotten the upper hand in their relationships with their opposite gender. On his own I don't think a rooster would allow a hen to drag him out shopping on a Sunday afternoon during football season; he would not let her steal the comic section while he read the paper at the breakfast table; and hens would never wrangle from him the right to vote.

I sometimes wonder if we should revert to nature; let the roosters rule the roost, and put the world right. Then again, it is also within the natural order that male emperor penguins sit on their eggs in the freezing arctic while their mates hunt for food; and black widow spiders devour the male spider after sex. Perhaps there is something to be said for man rising above his animal roots after all.

Be this as it may, chicken is one of the more popular meats in the world today. There is no culture, other than those that ascribe quite strictly to vegetarianism that does not eat them regularly and with gusto. Perhaps this is because chickens are easy to raise and can be used to good effect in so many dishes.

Not Everything Tastes Like Chicken

When questioned about how rattlesnake tastes, one often hears the word "chicken." I have never eaten rattlesnake; so I cannot vouch for the veracity of this statement. I have, though, had the courage to taste a variety of other seldom-eaten meats, and I must confess that I have never eaten anything I thought tasted quite like chicken. Chicken has a taste all its own and each part of the bird also has its subtle difference.

The breast has a different flavor than the leg or the thigh and the heart has a different texture than the wing. No wonder people say that everything from frog legs to iguanas taste like chicken—there are so many tastes in chicken to choose from. To get the full benefit of every part of a chicken, try roasting a chicken whole. This is one of the easiest and, at the same time, most elegant ways to cook chicken. This recipe can also be used for almost any other fowl.

Roast Chicken

Serving Size: 8
Preparation Time: 10 minutes
Ingredients:
1 whole chicken
1 dash pepper

This has got to be one of the easiest recipes in the world. At the same time it can be quite impressive.

Clean and wash chicken. Most of the time this also involves pulling the neck and liver and other pieces of anatomy out of the cavity of the chicken. Try not to think of biology class in high school. Just think succulent, tender and juicy—you'll be all right.

Place chicken in baking pan. It is best if the chicken can be raised on a grill. Sprinkle pepper over all. Jab holes in the chicken's skin with a sharp knife and LOOSELY cover with foil. This foil should merely be bent in the middle and should not be tucked in all the way around the pan.

Bake all at 375° for approximately 2½ to 3 hours.

Suggested Beer: Carling's Black Label.

Serving Ideas: Serve with boxed au gratin rice and — dare I say — broccoli.

Note: You may also wish to put paprika or salt on the skin. Even some parsley or basil or garlic. Barbecue sauce is good too.

Chicken Cordon Bleu

Chicken Cordon Bleu is a dish designed to dispel pansy notions about chicken preparation. This is a meal that requires the chicken be thoroughly beaten with a hammer. The procedure is impressive even though it is ostensibly accomplished after the chicken is dead. You don't need a hammer to kill a chicken. To really prove your manhood, wringing its neck will suffice. Some prefer merely choking the chicken. However, this can be a messy and embarrassing procedure if accomplished in public.

Admittedly, Cordon Bleu is not the easiest dish to make. Yet, it is worth the trouble and violence required. Cordon Bleu tastes great and has the added benefit of having a French sounding name that you didn't make up. Your girlfriend will have heard of this one before and will be shocked at your ability to put this together.

Make the most of the situation. Serve this meal with candlelight. It is one of the few meals that you should actually go through the trouble of selecting a wine. If your spouse is sophisticated, this is a dangerous maneuver. Be careful not to get a German wine. To be safe, don't buy anything that comes in a brown bottle or seems to require that you clear your throat in order to read the label, and buy nothing that you would have bought in college that begins with the letters *MD* and is fondly remembered with the appellation, "Mad Dog." Instead, get something that comes in one of those tall green bottles. Chardonnay is good. Even though it sounds French, an American male can pronounce the word without lisping and having his wrist go limp. There is nothing worse than sounding like a girl when you are trying to impress the little woman.

Chicken Cordon Bleu

Serving Size: 4
Preparation Time: 40 minutes
Ingredients:
2 chicken breasts without skin—boned
4 slices ham
4 slices Swiss cheese
4 slices cheddar cheese
½ cup breadcrumbs
1 dash pepper
½ tablespoon parsley
¼ tablespoon basil
½ teaspoon garlic powder
¼ teaspoon rosemary

Cut breasts in half along the sternum. Place each piece separately into a plastic bag and then pound it flat with a hammer. Sprinkle a light layer of breadcrumbs on a flat baking pan. Lay smashed piece of chicken on top of breadcrumbs. Place slice of ham on the chicken, and layer on the two cheeses.

Roll the result or at least fold it in half. Secure with a toothpick. Spread on spices, then spread on the remaining breadcrumbs. Bake in oven at 375° for about 45 minutes or until the scattered breadcrumbs start to turn black—this is a good indicator that the chicken is also done.

Suggested Wine: A white one.

Serving Ideas: Wild rice, or tame herb and butter rice if you can't catch the wild stuff.

Meat Pies

My chicken potpie is really a variant on the beef pot-pie recipe. I hope that I am not leaving myself open to accusations of unmanliness by saying that I prefer the chicken to the beef in this case.

The idea of meat pies has always intrigued me. Pies are usually thought of as sweets and eaten at dessert. So when someone mentions a meat pie, the assembled audience immediately thinks of mincemeat and crinkles up their collective nose as if they had just gotten a whiff of sodium sulfate. I make all due assurances that a chicken potpie contains no sweeteners and, since it contains a ubiquitous can of mushroom soup, must be delicious.

Meat pies seem to me to be typically English. The English will make a pie out of almost anything, even cuts of meat that you would only consider if you had survived a plane crash in the Andes and the flight attendants had all been wiped out. Take kidney pie for example and pork pie hats and four-and-twenty blackbirds. . . .

Chicken Potpie

Serving Size: 6
Preparation Time: 30 minutes
Ingredients:
1 chicken breast
1 potato
½ onion
1 carrot
3 mushrooms
1 can mushroom soup
1 dash pepper
½ tablespoon basil
½ tablespoon parsley
1 teaspoon oil
½ cup peas—frozen or fresh
1 pie crust

Put oil in pan on medium heat. Cut up chicken breasts and toss into pan. Clean and cut the vegetables (I think mushroom constitutes a vegetable, or maybe it is a fungus) into chunks. Throw vegetables (except peas) into pan along with spices. When the chicken is brown, dump in the mushroom soup and frozen peas. Stir vigorously.

Dump entire contents of pan into pie shell— cover over with pie dough either solid or crosshatched. Put in oven at 375° for 45 minutes to an hour.

Suggested Beer: Colt 45.

Serving Ideas: This is good with white rice.

Shake-and-Bake

Chicken is generally considered to be the healthiest of the meats we commonly eat. Much of this belief relies on the preparation. The fact is there is a tremendous amount of fat on any bird. Most of the fat, though, is immediately beneath the skin and is easily removed with the skin. For this reason, it is best to eat skinless chicken. My wife generally insists that the chicken also be boneless.

Chicken meat does not need all of the marbling that is necessary for beef. In fact—in most preparations—grease is not required at all. A quick, easy and healthy dish to spring on your wife is Oven-Fried Chicken. This is my variation of "shake-and-bake." Only there is no shaking—unless you are into that sort of thing.

Oven-Fried Chicken

Serving Size: 4
Preparation Time: 15 minutes
Ingredients:
4 chicken breast halves without skin
¼ cup breadcrumbs
¼ teaspoon pepper
¼ teaspoon garlic powder
1 teaspoon parsley
½ teaspoon basil
¼ teaspoon paprika

Sprinkle a light layer of breadcrumbs on a baking pan or cookie sheet. Flop down chicken breasts.

Don't be intimidated by the long list of spices here or even their measurements. Simply sprinkle spices over the chicken. You can vary the spices too.

Try adding lemon pepper, Parmesan cheese or oregano for a bit of variety. Sprinkle more breadcrumbs over the top of all.

Stick in oven at 376.5 degrees, or somewhere close to that temperature for about 45 minutes.

Suggested Wine: Miller Genuine Draft.

Serving Ideas: Good with potatoes or rice with any green vegetable.

Curry Favor

Here in America, we live in what has come to be called a melting pot of cultures. Although this fact has many political ramifications, with different factions vying for the vote of various sub-cultures, for me it has a far more important meaning. You see, every culture that has come to this country has brought with it, not simply a religion or a worldview, but a whole different array of foods.

Imagine how boring this place would be without pizza, tacos or chop soy. Well, these dishes may have had their roots in other cultures, but they have become as American as apple pie, and that is what living in a melting pot is really all about. It is not an effort to preserve purified each wave of national immigrants to this country. It is, rather, all of those influences melding naturally into one greater America.

It is with this optimistic perspective that I have personally adopted Chicken Curry as my own contribution to American culture. No, I am not from India; I don't even know anyone with Indian heritage. Heck, truth be known, I stole this recipe from my sister. I do know, however, that this is a great dish.

Besides its ethnic flavor, Chicken Curry is quite hot—in the spicy sense—and makes a great natural analgesic. It will clear blocked nasal passages quicker than you can say "Neo-Sinephrin." So serve this with plenty of Kleenexes and a cold glass of milk.

Chicken Curry

Serving Size: 8
Preparation Time: 40 minutes
Ingredients:
½ cup honey
¼ cup mustard
2 tablespoons butter
1 onion
½ tablespoon garlic powder
1½ tablespoons crushed red pepper
2 teaspoons curry powder
½ teaspoons ground ginger
8 chicken thighs
6 potatoes
4 carrots
4 fresh mushrooms

You need a good-sized 9×17-inch pan for this operation. Place chicken thighs—tastes better if they have not been skinned, even if it is not as healthy—in pan and pop into oven at 375°.

Clean and slice vegetables and set aside.

Put all remaining ingredients, including the onions, into a saucepan and bring to a boil—simmer for a few minutes. (Besides flavoring chicken, this concoction can be used to stain wood projects—works well on oak and pine.)

By this time, the chicken will have cooked some, though not thoroughly. Take it out of the oven and add all of the vegetables and pour the spice concoction over the top of all.

Cover tightly with a foil or in a Dutch oven. Then put back in oven and cook for about 2 hours. The chicken should fall apart when touched by a fork.

Suggested Beer: Any cold beer in a chilled mug. Milk is good too.

Serving Ideas: Stand-alone meal.

Stuffing and Dressing

Just so you will not fear that I have gotten too far away from recipes containing mushroom soup, I thought I would throw one in for good measure.

I am sure that you have sat down at Thanksgiving dinner and argued with friends and family over politics, work, metaphysics and various other topics. Though these topics change from year to year, there is one perennial discussion that returns with every traditional Thanksgiving meal. It revolves around the question: What is the difference between stuffing and dressing?

Truth is there is no difference in the ingredients; the difference is in the preparation. Stuffing to be stuffing must, in effect, be stuffed, crammed, rammed, shoved, squeezed or even coaxed into the cavity of a bird or at least between two halves of the same hunk of meat. The reason for calling it stuffing is as obvious as the reason cramming a basketball through the hoop at close range is called stuffing. Technically, if there is not a certain amount of grunting and arm flexing during this procedure, it is not stuffing.

Dressing, on the other hand, is like a three point jumper. It's a graceful arc straight from the pan and onto the plate. It is all net, no need to even touch the rim or the backboard. Grunting, however, is permissible.

Dressing is one of those dishes that are generally saved for the holidays. This is, perhaps, too limited a use. Dressing can add a bit of class to any meal. I tend to make it at least once a month, just because I get a craving for it. My wife and I, however have a difference of opinion about what is the best kind of dressing. I like corn bread stuffing and she likes the standard flavor.

This difference in taste also reflects differences in our personalities. She is quite reserved and I tend to be corny whenever the opportunity presents itself.

I generally make stuffing or dressing or whatever you want to call it, from the box. Petrified breadcrumbs and a little packet of spices come in the box. Even the economy brands of stuffing are quite good, however, they lack something in that they have no fresh vegetables. You can add any number of items to dressing (boxed or otherwise)—my suggestions include: onions, celery, carrots, almond slices, escargot (if you live in the Pacific Northwest) and a moderate number of potatoes. I frequently throw in whatever I happen to have standing by in the refrigerator.

If you want to be a purist and make your dressing from scratch, more power to ya! However you make it, here is a way to put it to good use.

Chicken and Dressing

Serving Size: 6
Preparation Time: 30 minutes
Ingredients:
2 chicken breasts—without skin
1 box stuffing
1 onion
1 carrot
1 can mushroom soup
3 dashes paprika

Chop onion and carrot. Prepare dressing per instructions, only toss in the onion and carrot as you are waiting for the water to boil. Set aside the dressing.

Cut chicken (turkey or pork may be substituted at your discretion) into strips. Dump dressing into long baking pan and mound it up in the middle of the pan. Line surrounding area with chicken strips, then spread the mushroom soup over the top of all. Sprinkle on the paprika.

Cover with lid or foil. Pop into oven for 1¼ hours at 375°.

Suggested Beer: Rainier.

Serving Ideas: Serve with broccoli, if you are into that kind of thing.

Centrifugal Entropy

My wife, Robin, professes to hate oriental food, yet her favorite meal is, beyond all doubt, chicken teriyaki. There is much danger in a spouse or a girlfriend proclaiming that something you prepare is her favorite. Especially if it happens to be something that is—as far as my recipes go—fairly time consuming.

If she likes it enough, she will be asking for the same meal repeatedly, and you will be stuck making it, because there is no denying a pleading woman when she has her heart set on chicken teriyaki. The key to avoiding this vicious cycle lies in mastering the devious art of sublime centrifugal entropy. Don't be put off by the scientific title; you have undoubtedly practiced this ancient marshal art in your spare time at home and not even realized it. It basically involves spreading chaos wherever you roam. When you come home from a hard day's work, you shed your shoes, your tie, your jacket and other miscellany in the most convenient corner. Your wife has chastised you for this behavior, but you profess to be incapable of controlling your actions. The same can be done while cooking. With chicken teriyaki you can spill rice from the package onto the floor, scatter bean sprouts over the stove as you stir fry, sprinkle teriyaki sauce inadvertently into the sugar bowl, or any number of other creative mess-making activities.

"This is all well and good," you say, "but who is going to clean up these little messes?"

This is the sublime part. You will make an effort to clean, but will prove once and for all that the Y chromosome is indeed missing the clean gene. I don't have to feign this ineptness for cleanliness and order; it comes naturally to me.

The result will either be a court settlement whereby you give up the kids, the house and whatever pocket change you have collected in jars over the years, or you will come to an arrangement similar to the one that my wife and I have made. Because I am so bad at cleaning, my wife insists on performing this duty. In addition, she lets me choose the meals, because she knows the entropic effect will be far less if I am making what I want. However, she likes teriyaki so much that, in spite of the mess, we have it every Sunday evening.

I find it curious that this is also the night she generally claims to have a headache and I get stuck with the dishes. You don't suppose she is practicing her own subtle art?

"Nah."

Chicken Teriyaki

Serving Size: 4
Preparation Time: 1 hour
Ingredients:
1½ cups rice
1 pound chicken thighs
2 carrots
5 mushrooms
1 onion
4 tablespoons teriyaki sauce
2 tablespoons soy sauce
1 tablespoon margarine
1 pound bean sprouts

Place dash of oil in large skillet and turn on medium-high. Cut up chicken and toss into skillet.

Put 3 cups of water and margarine in separate pan. Bring to boil. Add rice. Stir and set on simmer.

Add teriyaki sauce to the chicken. Cut up vegetables and mushrooms and fry with the chicken.

When rice is done, add bean sprouts to chicken. Turn frying pan on high and cook until most of water has evaporated.

Put rice on plate. Spoon teriyaki chicken on top. Serves four unless you are with my wife. In that case it serves two.

Suggested Beverage: Saki or any Japanese beer.
Serving Ideas: Serve with snow peas.

Barley: The Forgotten Grain

You have heard of beef barley soup. You may have even tried it once in your adventurous youth when you were sowing your wild oats, but this is likely the extent of your acquaintance with barley. It is incredible to me how few dishes there are that include this inexpensive yet delicious grain. Barley has a distinctive flavor and texture that is like nothing else, and until you have tried it separate from its beef soup companion, you do not know what you are missing.

Barley was once a staple crop in much of Western Europe, and is still eaten by some. However, in this country, the grain is all but ignored. This has happened because barley is not an exotic food in most people's minds and is too closely associated with our Anglo-Scottish heritage—which is shunned by many as oppressive, imperialistic and worst of all, bland. People sometimes forget that it was in Western Europe that modern democracy was born, nurtured and flourished. They forget that it has been Western Europe and America where ideals of individual freedoms and rights have been defended from onslaughts in two world wars and a bitter cold one. They forget that it has been western science and productivity that has brought the world into a wondrous age of information and plenty. I ask you: What right have we to shun our heritage? By what crooked reasoning is barley ignored?

I, for one, shall not ignore it, I praise it to the skies, and you will too when you try it with chicken in this recipe.

Chicken and Barley

Serving Size: 6
Preparation Time: 25 minutes
Ingredients:
1 cup barley
1 can chicken broth
1¼ cups water
1 onion
4 fresh mushrooms
2 tablespoons parsley
1 tablespoon basil
1 dash pepper
6 chicken thighs without skin
1 tablespoon margarine or butter

Dump the cup of barley into a baking dish. Pour broth and water over all. Add chopped onion and chopped mushrooms. Toss in spices and butter and mix all briefly with a spoon—or your finger if you insist.

Place pieces of chicken over all, cover, and place in oven at 375° for approximately 1½ hours or until the barley has absorbed all of the water and broth.

Do NOT force this dish on sensitive dinner guests; they might accuse you of being an imperialist.

Suggested Wine: Any ale will do nicely.

Serving Ideas: Serve with a green vegetable.

A Barbecue Secret

Secret recipes are intriguing. They lend an air of mystery to the cook or chef. If I have any cooking secrets, it is only because the world in general has not bothered to listen or I have neglected to tell them. I have often wondered what prompts people to keep a recipe secret. Does it increase their sense of their own importance, or will someone be hurt physically or emotionally by a revelation that someone put cinnamon in their meat loaf? Well, that at least is a possibility.

As far as I can figure, there is only one reason to have a secret in cooking: there is something disgusting about the cooking procedure or one of the ingredients. For example, my wife is blissfully unaware that there is mustard in Chicken Curry. Although she loves the stuff now, this knowledge would keep her from taking another bite of it. There would be little point in writing a cookbook if I were not willing to reveal my secrets and generally lay bare my soul.

So as long as I am not keeping secrets here, and am endeavoring to be completely open and honest, I must admit to having stolen the basic procedure for this next recipe from my brother, who is an excellent barbecuer in his own right. Let me just add that while I am being honest, I am not being generous as the only remuneration my brother shall receive is a few lines of text and a plate of barbecue chicken.

Barbecue Chicken

Serving Size: 6
Preparation Time: 30 minutes
Ingredients:
6 half chicken breasts—boneless and skinless
12 tablespoons barbecue sauce
6 tablespoons honey
2 dashes red pepper
2 dashes pepper
1 dash garlic powder
1 sprinkle of dried chives

Any real man will already know how to do this, but if you are still earning your stripes, here is the lowdown. (Here comes the secret.) If you have a charcoal grill first boil the chicken to be sure the insides get done. (For most gas grills with a hood this step will not be necessary).

Toss the chicken on the grill. Spread honey and barbecue sauce over the chicken. Liberally add spices. Turn as needed (usually not more than twice).

Suggested Beer: This is good with a light beer, like Coors. This may be dumped over the fowl during the cooking process depending on taste and the number of six-packs available.

Peace in Our Time

Wars have raged on since the dawn of humanity. There have been wars over corn liquor (the Whiskey Rebellion), wars over religion (the Thirty-Years' War and the Crusades), wars of conquest (most of the rest of them), and, not surprisingly, wars over women (the Trojan war, for example). Yet, I believe that wars have a root cause that underlies all of the superficial reasons given in the history books. It is a burning hunger, a lack of fulfillment, a space in the stomach and the mind that has been left empty and barren.

I am convinced that there is an end, a solution to war. If we could just serve a nicely baked chicken in a creamy Gorgonzola sauce to all of the world's leaders and military men, we would fill the empty place in the marshal soul of man. The soldiers would lay down their arms. Politicians would kiss each other on the cheek in brotherly affection. We would indeed achieve peace in our time.

I base this revolutionary theory on the fact that Gorgonzola cheese is a blue cheese that comes out of Italy. The Italians are noted lovers and also have made fairly poor soldiers ever since the fall of the Roman Empire. Historians generally considered their energies as having been spent in the rise of the Empire and the precipitous plunge into decadence. However, the truth is that they discovered Chicken Gorgonzola and have been unable to mount a creditable fighting force ever since.

Chicken Gorgonzola

Serving Size: 4
Preparation Time: 30 minutes
Ingredients:
4 chicken breast halves
2 tablespoons margarine or butter
2 tablespoons flour
1 cup milk
1 dash pepper
½ cup Gorgonzola cheese

It is best if the chicken is skinless and boneless. Place chicken in a baking dish, sprinkle on pepper. Cover the dish and place in the oven at about 375° for about an hour or until chicken is cooked through and tender.

When chicken is about done, put margarine or butter in saucepan on medium heat. When margarine begins to bubble, stir in flour. Make sure you get the flour completely wet with the margarine. Immediately add milk, crumbled cheese and pepper. Keep on medium heat and stir fairly constantly until sauce is thickened.

Put chicken on plates and dump sauce over the top.

If you cannot find Gorgonzola cheese, try bleu cheese.

Recommended Beer: Bass Ale.

Hoi Poloi

Many of the recipes we now take for granted were at one time not eaten by *hoi poloi*, us denizens of the lower classes, us proletarians. Because the ingredients were costly and the tastes expensive, only the wealthy could afford dishes such as *pheasant picant por la duk*, or what not. Indeed, the peasant was so heavily taxed that he could barely throw together some recipe like chicken and barley, and was more likely to be eating gruel morning, noon and night. Now gruel is fine stuff as far as it goes, but it gets tiresome after a few years.

As the industrial revolution and the division of labor brought wealth to the lowest classes, all could enjoy meals that once had been reserved for only the most highfalutin. Such a meal is Chicken a la King. Of course, a real man would not want to be caught concocting such a fabrication. We are more down-to-earth, and don't need to indulge ourselves in the delicacies of past ages. It is better to think of Chicken a la King as a chicken in gravy sauce. Pour it over a few hardy biscuits and tell your friends it's chipped chicken on a roll. Only you need know — you are eating like a king.

Chicken a la King or Chicken with Gravy

Serving Size: 4
Preparation Time: 30 minutes
Ingredients:
2 chicken breasts—boneless without skin
1 tablespoon vegetable oil
1 dash pepper
1 dash salt
1 dash garlic powder
4 tablespoons margarine
4 tablespoons flour
1½ cups milk
2 slices Swiss cheese
2 scoops sour cream
1 carrot
1 cup frozen peas

This is one of those dishes that is a fair amount of work, but may be worth the trouble. Cut chicken breast into bite sized hunks. In a frying pan on medium heat put oil, spread it around, then dump in the chicken. Slice carrots into penny sized pieces. Sprinkle on spices and fry until chicken is done through.

Dump chicken into a separate bowl. Now add margarine to frying pan. Let it melt, then add flower. When flour is all soaked with the butter, add milk. Stir pretty much continuously until the sauce thickens. Dump back the chicken and carrots.

Add sour cream, cheese and peas. Let it cook for about five minutes—at least long enough for the peas to warm through. Taste. If needed, add more spices.

Serving Ideas: This "a la King" stuff can be served over rice or biscuits or noodles or whatever happens to take your fancy.

Versatility

You may have noticed in the above recipes that chicken is a versatile meat. Not only can it be used in a variety of dishes but also it can be substituted for other meats in any number of recipes. Where recipes call for hamburger, ground chicken can do just as well. Also, I have used pork to substitute for chicken in some recipes. Try pork in the chicken and dressing recipe. The only thing to be careful about is spice. Certain spices are typical with chicken, especially thyme. Also, I am not fond of chicken with any kind of marinara sauce. However, this is a personal thing that derives from a bad experience of my youth when my own dear father decided to experiment with food preparation. His concoction included spaghetti sauce, chicken, corn, green olives and cottage cheese. I do not think he could have chosen a more unlikely combination. Before you experiment too wildly with food, you should have some degree of experience and perhaps a license from the Food and Drug Administration. After we ate his meal, I believe that we were eligible for funding from the Department of the Interior for toxic waste cleanup.

Chicken can be the foundation of a wonderful meal. I shall conclude the chicken chapter with a once savored, but now oft-ignored recipe for chicken. Don't worry — there is no tomato sauce in this one.

Chicken and Dumplings

Servings: 6
Preparation Time: 30 minutes
Ingredients:
1½ pounds chicken breast
1 tablespoon oil
1 dash pepper
1 dash salt
1 teaspoon crushed parsley
1 teaspoon crushed basil
1 cup frozen peas
2 cut carrots
4 mushrooms
1 onion—for dumplings
2 cups flour
4 teaspoons baking powder
2 eggs
½ cup milk
1 dash of pepper
1 dash of parsley

First, cut up the chicken and toss it into a good-sized pot (preferably one with a lid) along with the oil. Fry the chicken, cut up onions, carrots, cut mushrooms and spices until the chicken is no longer raw.

While the chicken is frying, throw the dumpling ingredients together into a bowl and stir thoroughly.

When chicken is done, add peas and about ½ cup water. In a small cup mix 2 tablespoons of flower with about ¼ cup water. Bring water and chicken to a boil. While stirring, dump in flour and water mixture. This will thicken the broth. Now turn the pot down to simmer and spoon out dumpling mixture over the top. Place lid on pan and cook until dumplings are done. This could take as long as an hour or as little as a half-hour, depending on your stove.

OTHER MEATS

The Other White Meat and Other White Meats

For good or for evil, every barnyard animal has a reputation. If cows—especially bulls—are tough, even masculine, and chickens are cowardly or flighty, then pigs have an even more entrenched stereotype. This stereotype is one that the pro-hog lobby has not been able to dispel in spite of all its public service announcements and donations to key congressmen. You see, pigs have a reputation for gluttony.

Of all the vices ascribed to pigs, perhaps the most unsavory is piggishness. Besides having made the top seven of the famous deadly sins, it is also considered to be bad form, even unfashionable, to be a hog. This makes the swine the pariah of modern society. To be unfashionable is worse, perhaps, than being labeled a thief or an ax-murderer.

Unfortunately for the pig, its barnyard stereotype is basically true. Indeed, Gertrude Stein's famous statement about roses would have had more meaning had it been made about pigs. *A pig is a pig*. No doubt about it. However, when we sit down to the table with a chop or a ham slice, the personality of the pig matters not. For by the mysterious magic of the culinary arts this creature is transformed into a delectable food known as pork. As with chicken, one need not be afraid that the character of the creature being consumed will somehow find its way into the psyche of the consumer.

Besides having acquired a reputation for sloth and gluttony, the poor pig is further stuck with being a ham. I believe a ham is someone who imposes his absurd sense of humor on the mass of humanity around him. I can comprehend most of the barnyard stereotypes, but this one is beyond my understanding, as I have never seen a pig ham it up — so to speak.

In any case, ham is one of those meats, like sausage, that have been cured or smoked. For this reason, it can sit in the refrigerator for an age, though not infinitely, and still be good.

You can also buy imitation hams. I even recommend them. As far as I am concerned, a turkey ham, if it has enough fat, is as good as ham made in the traditional manner.

Perhaps the best thing about ham is that the curing process has killed all of the germs and has, in essence, slow-cooked the meat. This means that ham does not have to be cooked before it is consumed. You can expedite a slice directly from the ham-bone to the deep pit of your stomach, pausing along the way only to tingle a few taste buds.

Ham has a nice smoked flavor that adds much to any dish. Try it in a salad or in an omelet — fried straight up — or try out my creamed ham and noodle recipe.

Ham and Cream Sauce

Serving Size: 4
Preparation Time: 20 minutes
Ingredients:
2 slices ham
½ onion
1 dash garlic powder
1 dash pepper
2 tablespoons margarine or butter
2 tablespoons flour
1 cup milk
12 ounces egg noodles
1 tablespoon oil
½ cup frozen peas

Cube ham slices—hopefully these are thick ham slices. Chop onions. Fry onions in oil until slightly softened.

On medium heat, place margarine in frying pan. When this bubbles, add flour and mix thoroughly. Add milk and stir until sauce thickens. Add ham and onions and frozen peas. Add spices.

Prepare egg noodles as per directions on the package. Egg noodles get done pretty quickly, so you might want to keep a close eye on these fellows.

When egg noodles are soft, strain in calendar. Flop noodles on plate, pour on sauce, you're ready to eat.

Recommended Beverage: Hamms Beer.

Luck of the Draw

I seldom sit back and think to myself, "Now, what am I going to make for supper?" Instead, I go to the freezer and pull out the first package of meat that my grimy mitts come across. With this in hand, I decide what it can be made into. Very frequently and often to my surprise, a package of pork appears before my eyes. I like pork, but I seldom associate it directly with supper or dinner or whatever.

Luckily, there are many things that can be done with pork. In fact, most recipes for chicken and many of the ones for beef can be made with pork instead. Try pork and dressing with the mushroom soup sauce (instead of chicken and dressing) or a pork roast instead of a roast beast. However, there are other dishes that are traditionally made with pork. Most notably, pork chops. There are several ways to pre-pare pork chops, you can fry them in a pan, cook them on the grill and, my favorite, bread them and bake them.

Breaded Pork Chops

Serving Size: 4
Preparation Time: 10 minutes
Ingredients:
4 pork chops
6 tablespoons breadcrumbs
1 dash pepper
1 dash parsley
1 dash basil
1 tablespoon dried onions

My wife insists that I lay down a layer of alumi-num foil in the base of a baking pan before I begin. It saves her some scrubbing down the road.

Sprinkle a layer of breadcrumbs over the foil and lay pork chops on top of them. Dash on the spices, then sprinkle on the rest of the breadcrumbs.

Put in oven at 400°. Bake for 30-45 minutes.

Serving Ideas: Good with peas, boiled potatoes and cottage cheese.

Preferred Beverage: Labatts.

Euro-Pork

European dishes are always in style. This is because Europeans make food their life. Every European nation has its specialties and every tiny nation has its chefs who lovingly prepare every dish with little fingers raised. They also work with their nose condescendingly stuck into the air, and despite these handicaps they crank out some great stuff.

Now that Europe is combining into one huge conglomerated mass, their food may go the same way. This is a disappointment to some. Yet there are already benefits coming from this amalgamation of cultures: Euro-Pork. This dish is quick, elegant and involves slabs of meat.

Euro-Pork

Serving Size: 4
Preparation Time: 15 minutes
Ingredients:
4 pieces boneless pork top loin—beaten
1 tablespoon olive oil
1 tablespoon chives—diced
1 tablespoon parsley
1 teaspoon basil
½ cup Madeira
1 dash salt
1 dash pepper

Beat a few boneless pork chops or whatnot into a senseless pulp with hammer—or don't—it's not absolutely necessary but it is a good way to take out your frustrations. Dump olive oil in a pan and heat it up a bit (medium heat is usually enough) and then put chops in, dash with salt and pepper (this is essential). Fry the chops until they brown or caramelize. That is: make sure there is some brown stuff stuck to the bottom of the pan. Don't worry; you won't have to scrape it out later.

Remove chops. Add chives, parsley and basil to the brown stuff on the bottom and let it heat for about 30 seconds or a minute. Then add the Madeira. Stir it around while still heating until most—but not all—of the wine has boiled away. Then dump the resulting sauce on the pork chops. It's now ready to go. This is one of the few quick meat, entree recipes, and this stuff cools fast—so make sure everything else is done about the time you start this dish.

WARNING: Do not put the Madeira in the pan at the same time the chops are there. For some reason the results yield an unpleasant mushiness to the pork.

Suggested Wine: Any beer from a green bottle.

Serving Ideas: Good with rice. Farmhouse broccoli and cheese is good.

Country Style

Country style is an appellation I have frequently pondered. As you may have already guessed, I frequently ponder many inconsequential topics. In any case, "country style" gets attached to any number of dishes. Of course, it hints that the recipe was, is, and always will be one that is used on the farm in the American Midwest, somewhere near the plains of Kansas. One would also expect it to be plentiful and filling and loaded with fat.

These, at any rate, are the attributes that I expect and even desire. It is interesting to note that most of the people I know who live in the country eat a more "healthy" diet, lentils, vegetables and dandelion weeds. It is a fairly unpalatable regimen if you ask me. Well, I at least will not disappoint your expectations for a country style meal.

Country Style Spare Ribs

Serving Size: 8
Preparation Time: 15 minutes
Ingredients:
1½ pounds boneless pork spare ribs
1 jar barbecue sauce
1 tablespoon dried onions
1 dash garlic
1 dash pepper
6 tablespoons honey

Acquire a raised rack and place in baking pan. Lay in spare ribs. Spread honey on pork and the sauce over the honey—no need to use the whole jar here. Pile it on and spread it around with a fork. Sprinkle on the spices.

Place in oven at 392° for a little over an hour. Check it frequently beginning at the 45-minute mark, at which time—depending on how much you like it—you may wish to spread on some more barbecue sauce.

The pork is done when it looks a little dry and it is cut easily with a fork.

Serving Ideas: Serve with baked potatoes and peas.

You Can Tune a Piano, But You Can't Tuna Fish

Fish, of all varieties, is definitely manly fare. Yet I have, for the most part, neglected it. This is easily explained by the fact that I am allergic to fresh fish. Unable to experiment with fish in recipes, I feel it is perhaps better if I leave the topic alone.

It is also important to note that fish is brain food. My friends and family feel that my inability to eat fish might explain a lot. However, I wistfully feel it only points up what I might have been.

Sly insults aside, there is one fish to which I have never had an allergic reaction. That is tuna fish. This is one of the more versatile as well as inexpensive foods that can be drawn from a tin can. You may substitute canned chicken in nearly any recipe that calls for tuna, but considering cost as well as taste, I see little reason to do so.

One of the easiest dishes known to the culinary arts is tuna and noodle casserole. This one is good to throw together on a Saturday afternoon during the final four. You can sit on the couch next to your favorite potato mate with a full bowl of tuna and noodle casserole and know that you are getting a wallop of nutrition coupled with a nice blast of brain food to help you keep track of who is where in the standings.

Tuna and Noodle Casserole

Serving Size: 6
Preparation Time: 20 minutes
Ingredients:
1 can tuna in water
1 can mushroom soup
1 package egg noodles
1 tablespoon margarine
½ cup frozen peas
1 dash pepper

Boil a good-sized pan of water. Add egg noodles. It is important to remember that egg noodles get done much more quickly than regular pasta noodles, so test them for doneness often and early. When noodles are soft, strain out water.

Dump noodles back into pan. Drain water off from tuna fish. Add all ingredients and return to medium heat until mixture is hot.

Roofing Material

Some of the best recipes are made from the simplest of ingredients. Many go back generations to a time before our reckoning. These recipes are steeped in tradition and every bite recalls a less stressful time. You have probably heard of "Slop-on-the-Shingle" or some variant. When I was a child, I always heard it referred to by its acronym: "S.O.S." I can remember watching a movie where a ship was going down in heavy seas. From the radio room, they sent out the Morse code message, "S . . . O . . . S." I thought they were placing an order for when they returned to port.

Of course, "slop" is merely the polite term many mothers used to replace the original appellation, which will go unmentioned here. When you recall cedar shingles and you see a stack of toast topped with gravy, it is easy to see how this culinary delight got its name.

S.O.S. makes a filling lunchtime meal. It is easy to whip together and is a great hit with the little ones. Try it.

Slop-on-the-Shingle

Serving Size: 10
Preparation Time: 15 minutes
Ingredients:
1 can mushroom soup
1 can tuna in water
1 tablespoon margarine
10 slices bread

Empty the can of soup and tuna into saucepan. Add a couple tablespoons of water. Set on medium heat. Stir intermittently until the slop becomes hot.

Place shingles, *er . . .* I mean, bread in toaster. Butter bread when heated to your desire. Lay toast on plate ladle or dump on slop, sprinkle on salt and pepper to taste and there you have it.

Lamb

I'm not sure whether lamb constitutes another white meat. In the package it looks a lot like beef. I throw it into this section for lack of a better place. Mutton is a meat more commonly eaten in other parts of the world, most notably in the Mediterranean basin and other hilly highland regions where cattle do not fare well.

Sheep, lamb, mutton or whatever you choose to call it, has a rather pungent aftertaste. It can take you by surprise if you are unfamiliar with it. That's why so many people eat lamb with mint jelly. For my part, the only thing I like jelly on is my toast. Perhaps it is me, but whenever I cook lamb on the stove top it is tough and recalcitrant as a teenager with a cigarette drooping from his lips. It is best to approach lamb in the same manner you would a beef roast: cook it in a covered dish in the oven or try it on the barbecue.

Hey, just a side note of interest here. There are often two different words for the animals we eat. You know, lamb-mutton, pig-pork, cow-beef. The reason for this dichotomy has to do with the Norman Invasion of England almost 1000 years ago. It seems the French-Norman terms for these meats were adopted by the eating class, the conquerors, and the animal name was retained by those poor Saxons who had to tend the lowly animals. I would call the French-derived terms as pansyish if I didn't know those tough fellows ate their meat from the points of their swords.

Roast Lamb

Serving Size: 4
Preparation Time: 15 minutes
Ingredients:
4 lamb chops
4 potatoes
4 mushrooms
1 dash pepper
1 dash ground rosemary
1 dash basil
2 turnips

Place lamb chops in a covered dish. Sprinkle on spices. Put potatoes, turnips and mushrooms in pan. If you wish, you may add carrots and onions too. Cover pan with foil or lid.

Put into oven at 375° for 2 hours.

The Sausage Effect

It is a well-known precept of dietary science that various foods have various effects on the human digestive system. The problem is that these effects are not universal. My father insists that eating a banana is like sticking a cork in . . . well a relatively tender spot. Bananas have no such effect on me. As far as I am concerned, a banana is a fairly neutral food.

Thus any advice from me on the subject of natural diuretics is purely speculative. Nevertheless, I am certain that there is something out there known as the sausage effect. It is caused by the consumption of excessive amounts of sausage and leaves the body depleted and drained of energy. I am convinced that this effect is a direct result of fats and oils that have a tendency to grease the skids—if you know what I mean.

This is not to say that you should stay away from sausage. Far from it! I only caution you against over-indulging. I happen to love kielbasa or Polish sausage or what have you. There is a product called Cheddarwurst that is great on a bun with a little mayonnaise, mustard and catsup. There is another danger here, though. Polish sausage dogs tend to plump when microwaved or boiled. If not approached with respect and from the appropriate angle, one can be squirted in the nose by a hot stream of boiling oil; not a pleasant experience, I can tell you. And the subsequent blister will invite ridicule at least until the slow healing process is completed and possibly for some time thereafter.

Perhaps the best way to consume sausage is with sauerkraut. For a pleasant exposure to the sausage effect, try this recipe.

Sausage and Kraut

Serving Size: 6
Preparation Time: 15 minutes
Ingredients:
1 ring polish sausage
1 can sauerkraut
6 potatoes

Toss ring of sausage into baking dish. Clean potatoes and cut in half. Place potatoes carefully around the ring of sausage. Dump can of kraut, juice and all over the top of potatoes and sausage.

Cover with foil or lid. Cook in oven for about an hour at 375°.

Suggested Beer: Killian's Red—I know it's not German, but it tastes right.

Serving Ideas: Good with cottage cheese.

Turkey

There is no more substantial food than turkey. It is unfortunate that it is reserved primarily for holidays. You are probably already aware that turkeys are a bird native to North America. The Aztecs kept them much the same way Europeans kept chickens. In fact, it was turkey meat that fueled Cortez's army while it conquered Mexico. I find it interesting that we do not generally associate turkey with Mexico but with Plymouth Rock and the first Thanksgiving and all that.

One more historical note: Ben Franklin wanted the national bird to be the turkey because of its productivity, versatility and nativity. He was overruled by a bunch of guys who thought turkeys were not smart enough to be the national bird.

As far as I know, turkeys are no dumber than the average bird or even a few humans I am acquainted with. Nevertheless, Franklin was correct about the versatility of turkeys. Nowadays, we make ham and sausage and pepperoni and any number of meats from them. Ground turkey can also be used as a low fat substitute for hamburger. Besides roasting the bird whole, various parts can be used in various ways.

Barbecue Turkey Drumsticks

Servings: 6
Preparation Time: No time flat.
Ingredients:
6 turkey drumsticks
1 bottle of your favorite barbecue sauce
2 dashes pepper
1 dash garlic powder
1 dash salt
2 dashes red pepper

Place drumsticks on rack within a baking pan. Pour sauce on drumsticks; sprinkle on spices. Place in a 378° oven for about an hour—perhaps a tad longer depending on the size of the drumsticks.

Recommended Beverage: Fosters in the shade.

Serve with boiled potatoes sprinkled with bacon bits and a huge dollop of sour cream.

My Favorite Holiday

Most people have a favorite time of the year or a favorite holiday. Opinion polls are pretty much in agreement that the favorite holiday of children in the U.S. and Canada is Christmas. Both parents normally find Christmas to be too fatiguing and frantic to constitute a favorite. The favorite of most women — though feminists have struggled long and hard against this tendency — is St. Valentine's Day. Their reason is obvious.

Men, of course, disdain most holidays because of the need to remember to buy their wives flowers, a gift or jewelry — and if they happen not to remember, dire consequences will result. I am convinced that Scrooge was correct in his original assumptions about Christmas. He could equally have applied his apt phrase of "bah, humbug" to any number of other days in the year.

Most men will agree that the best holiday of the year is Thanksgiving. There are manifold reasons. First, he doesn't need to worry about gifts. Second, there are six hours of professional football featuring the Detroit Lions and the Dallas Cowboys. Third, it is the beginning of a four-day weekend. Four, hunting season has begun or soon will begin. Five, it is too cold to cut the grass and too warm for snow. Six, pumpkin pie. And finally, the clincher: green beer. No, wait, that's St. Patrick's Day. Anyway, there is sure to be one huge turkey with dressing and what is typically referred to as all the trimmings.

Turkey and Dressing and Trimmings

Serving Size: 10
Preparation Time: 1 hour 30 minutes
Ingredients:
1 turkey
6 ounces stuffing cubes
1 ounce almonds
1 onion
1 potato
1 carrot
3 tablespoons flour
1 dash pepper
1 teaspoon thyme
½ teaspoon rosemary
1 tablespoon parsley

Rinse turkey and pull out the customary sack of innards. Discard the liver, but throw the neck, heart, gizzards and any other part of the turkey you feel is edible into a saucepan. Boil the contents.

Meanwhile cut up onions, potatoes, carrots and almonds. When the meat in the saucepan has been cooked, remove the turkey innards. Hopefully, you will have about 2 cups of broth, if not, add water until you do. Add stuffing cubes, chopped vegetables and almonds and spices, stir. Cut up heart and gizzards and add to dressing. Stir again.

Stuff turkey by cramming the dressing into the cavity of the bird. Be sure to grunt or it will not be true stuffing.

With a sharp knife poke little holes in the bird in various places. Sprinkle on pepper.

Place turkey in baking dish chest side up. It is best if it is elevated slightly from the bottom of the pan by a grill. The grill, however, is not strictly required. Make a tent of a strip of aluminum foil and place over the bird. Place all in oven at 375°. This bird is going to have to cook for at least three and a half hours possibly five or six depending on size. You may have bought one with a thermometer—if so, it should be done when the thermometer pops. Without the thermometer, cut into the space between the leg and the breast. If there is an excess of clear juice there or uncooked blood, you know that you have a ways to go yet.

When turkey seems to be getting close to being done, remove drippings with a gravy ladle or a baster. Place the drippings in a saucepan and quickly put it in the freezer for about 15 minutes. This will harden up the fat enough to scrape it off the top with a spoon.

Place saucepan on the stove. Bring drippings to boil. Mix flour with water until it is the consistency of Elmer's Glue. Pour into boiling drippings while stirring. This commotion will create gravy.

When gravy is done, so should be the turkey and whatever other dishes you have prepared. Place ingredients on the table and demolish in ten minutes what it took five hours to create.

Suggested Beer: Michelob.

Serving Ideas: Good for Thanksgiving dinner.

Notes: If you require an estimate of how long a specific size bird will cook, the following table may be of assistance:

Size of Bird (lbs.)	Cooking Time (hrs.)
6-8	3-3½
8-12	3½-4
12-16	4-5
16-20	5-6
20-24	6-7
25+	Your oven is not big enough for this turkey.

How to Avoid the Post-Thanksgiving Letdown

It is remarkable how much effort a human will go through to achieve a few brief moments of satisfaction. Athletes work and struggle constantly to achieve a few moments of glory on the playing field. An artist spends hours in front of a canvas just so he can hear some critic say, "The ethno-concentric boundaries of his work fully express the primal nature of urban-living, while at the same time they feed the lofty urges of the soul." (Or words to that effect.) Even a man, if forced to it, will put up with hours of monotonous foreplay to achieve a few moments of genuine sexual gratification.

The fact of the matter is that almost anything worthwhile requires an investment of time and effort that, objectively viewed, seems out of all proportion to the final result. Thanksgiving dinner is a case in point. Indeed, as one surveys the table at the end of the traditional meal one wonders that so much preparation time could have turned into a field of debris in such a hurry. For the cook at such an occasion there is always a post-meal letdown. If you aren't the cook, therefore, you should praise this person for their efforts to the point of utter obsequiousness. If you are the chef, you should invite such abject adulation, if only to fire future efforts.

However you feel, it is well to reflect that all effort was not in vain. A great meal is like a great work of art, or a close football game. Though it may not last forever in the physical realm it will live in the hearts and minds of its participants until their dying day. Next year when everyone is gathering again for the great holiday everyone will recall the Thanksgiving they spent at your house and wonder how they could match that meal you threw together.

Then again, you might prepare a passable Thanksgiving meal the easy way. A turkey will roast just as well without stuffing. You may produce the dressing from a box, and Instant Potato buds are nearly indistinguishable from the real thing. Get your gravy from a jar and limit yourself to one vegetable, green beans come to mind. Tell someone else to bring dessert.

VEGETABLES AND SALADS

Vegetables

The average person, when asked to divulge their least favorite food, will usually name a vegetable. For George Bush, the former President of the United States, it was broccoli. I am fond of broccoli myself, but I can certainly understand where he acquired his distaste for the cruciform vegetable. The former President had been a pilot in the Navy. Having been in the Navy myself for a few years I was exposed to the manner in which Navy cooks treat vegetables. Everything is steamed or boiled until no flavor, texture or substance remains. This treatment is especially hard on broccoli, which is best when fresh and only lightly cooked.

I believe that the reason for this universal dislike for one or another vegetable is because, first, there is such a variety of vegetables to choose from; and second, a person is unwarrantedly exposed to unwanted vegetables more often than any other dish. For example, in a restaurant, one is seldom asked what vegetable they wish to have with their meal. It is generally provided without question. My wife is not a fan of zucchini, but she is confronted with it on a regular basis at our favorite restaurants. When it is set in a steaming heap before her she crinkles her nose and renews her vow of undying hatred for the vegetable. She seldom has the opportunity to express her dislike for, say, liver. No one has been foolish enough to set unasked-for liver before her while she is holding a fork and a sharp knife.

Recent studies show that the most favored vegetable is corn and the least is spinach. It has also been found that the most likely vegetable to stain your shirt red is the beet, and the most likely vegetable to come to life, exhibit human consciousness and be hurled at a passing stranger on a dusty road at dusk near a town called Sleepy Hollow is the asparagus. These results are exactly why I don't trust polling or scientific studies until they pass my personal sanity test.

Most fresh vegetables can be simply chopped up and shoved into the microwave for two to five minutes to be ready to be placed directly on the table to complement the main dish of your choice. Even frozen corn, peas or broccoli, blasted in the microwave, can be served with any of the entree's I prescribe in the first few chapters. Add a starch, like a potato or rice, and you have a passable meal. However, there will be times when you will want to spruce up a vegetable. This can be done by topping it with cheese or merely making a white sauce—which is described in the chapter on dips. Or you may try one of the recipes included in this chapter.

Broccoli and Cheese Sauce

Serving Size: 6
Preparation Time: 10 minutes
Ingredients:
1 can Campbell's Cheddar Cheese Soup
3 tablespoons sour cream
2 tablespoons milk
1 package frozen broccoli
1 dash pepper
1 dash garlic

Empty all ingredients except broccoli into a saucepan; cover. Heat on low, stirring frequently until concoction is hot. Add broccoli and heat until broccoli cooks through.

You can vary the amount of broccoli in this recipe to make it conform to your tastes.

Serving Ideas: Good as a topping on potatoes, mashed or baked.

Potluck

One of the more popular modes of social eating is known as the potluck. I am not certain where the term is derived from, but I would guess that it has something to do with the fact that what you finally end up eating is a matter of fortune, good or otherwise. That is the "luck" part; I will leave to you to figure out where the "pot" comes from.

In case you are a social outcast or, conversely, too highbrow to ever have participated in such a venture, I shall describe a potluck for you. A potluck is a gathering where every family or person brings a different dish. The type of dish a person contributes is usually designated based on the first initial of a last name. For some reason, I always seem to get saddled with dessert. Truth is, I am not a dessert man. The last potluck social I attended had a Mexican theme and I had no idea what dessert to bring. I ended up calling my sister who is usually resourceful in such cases. She advised me that sopapilla would be appropriate. I told her that I did not relish the idea of eating sofa pillows. I decided to bring ice cream instead. I should have taken her advice. At least sofa pillows don't melt before you have a chance to get to them.

In any case, no matter how small or how large a gathering of potluckers, there will always be at least one pot loaded with green bean casserole. Now, some people may scoff or even turn up their noses at green bean casserole, but it happens to be one of my favorite vegetables—and not just because one of the ingredients is mushroom soup. I actually look forward to potlucks, anticipating flopping a big pile of green beans on my plate next to the equally obligatory sliced ham and Jello salad. For some reason, no one ever makes these peculiar dishes for themselves; they wait for an opportune moment to spring them on someone else. Not that these foods are unappetizing, they simply need to be made in bulk and the ingredients are relatively inexpensive.

Potluck food is not half bad, as long as most of the participants are not devotees of the art of nouvelle cuisine. The atmosphere is generally laid-back, and as long as someone brings a deck of cards, a good time is had by all.

You don't have to wait for a potluck to enjoy its benefits. You can bake your own ham, put together a Jello salad and whip up your own green bean casserole. When you get your dishes prepared, grab a paper plate, plastic utensils and pile on as much as you can fit without the plate bending in half. Then grab a deck of cards out of the junk drawer. Even without company, you can always play solitaire. Yum, potluck for one.

Green Bean Casserole

Serving Size: 8
Preparation Time: 10 minutes
Ingredients:
2 cans green beans
1 can mushroom soup
1 onion
¼ cup bacon bits
1 dash pepper

This is pretty easy. Just open up all the cans, dump it all into a baking dish, add chopped onions. Sprinkle bacon bits on top. Pepper to taste. Cover. Shove into oven for about and hour at 375°. Bring to potluck.

Note: You can use dried onions in a can instead of a fresh chopped one.

Zucchini

Most vegetables are versatile. Zucchini is no exception. It can be sliced up and put into soups. It can be baked, fried, breaded and even skewered.

If you have never grown zucchini in your garden, then you probably think it is a thin narrow vegetable that resembles a cucumber that you often see on the grocer's vegetable stand. However, if you leave it on the vine long enough, it will take on the size and consistency of a baseball bat. I am sure it can be cooked in this state, but it is more fun to whack around a ball in the backyard with the kids.

Another factor in growing zucchini is its prolific nature. One plant can yield thousands, dare I say, millions of zucchini. To keep up with the production of your garden, you will have to cook zucchini day and night. Because it is so easy to come by in season, I find it difficult to break down and buy zucchini even when it is not in season. Being such a cheap—I mean—frugal fellow, I only eat zucchini two months out of the year. Don't let your frugality deter you from this excellent vegetable. Whether your zucchini is store bought or home grown, try this easy recipe.

Fried Zucchini

Serving Size: 4
Preparation Time: 10 minutes
Ingredients:
1 zucchini
1 tablespoon margarine or butter
1 dash salt
1 dash pepper
1 onion

Put frying pan on medium heat. Add margarine or butter. Slice the zucchini crosswise. Chop onions. When margarine has melted, add zucchini. Add spices to taste. Fry until zucchini is browned. Do not cover; it will make zucchini soggy.

This simple recipe also works for other vegetables such as summer squash and eggplant.

Asparagus

Most vegetables are not very expensive. I attribute this fact to modern agriculture's ability to cheaply and easily mass-produce, store and transport the average vegetable. There is, however, one vegetable that defies this rule. Asparagus is fairly expensive. I think this is because it takes several years to grow a decent crop and even then it is not easily harvested.

Asparagus is also a crop that really must be bought and consumed in season. A cook must be careful to get spears that are relatively tender because an asparagus spear that has been in the ground too long will have the taste and consistency of a nylon rope. Usually thinner spears are younger and tenderer. If possible, they should be stored with the sliced ends in water. If you are picking out asparagus at the store, stick a thumbnail into the base of a stalk. If it feels like the cane could support a line, a hook and a six-pound catfish, put it back.

When preparing spears, I always cut away at least and inch and sometimes more from the bottom. The bottom will turn to rope first and the transformation seems to move up the stem of the plant. If your asparagus has sat in the refrigerator for a few days, you will want to bite into a sample spear to find where the rough skin begins. Even if you are as cheap as I am, you might as well resign yourself to cutting off and discarding the ropy part. It's better than having everyone placing wet, green gobs on their plate at dinner.

For distinctive flavor, nothing beats asparagus. This distinction keeps it from being used in a whole lot of dishes, yet it will complement any dish, especially those in the white meat category.

Asparagus and Swiss Cheese Bake

Serving Size: 4
Preparation Time: 10 minutes
Ingredients:
1 pound asparagus
1 tablespoon margarine or butter
3 slices Swiss cheese
1 tablespoon parsley
1 dash paprika

Clean and slice asparagus into one-inch lengths. This is important; otherwise, if your wife is like mine, she will cut the spears in half when they come out of the oven, take the heads and leave you with the lower end of the stems. If they are already cut up and mixed up under a pile of cheese, this type of behavior is forestalled.

Place asparagus in baking pan with margarine or butter. Place Swiss cheese slices over top. (You can also use mozzarella.) Sprinkle on spices. Bake in a 350° oven for a half hour or so. A little longer or a little less will not hurt it.

Acorn Squash

The truth is most vegetable recipes are simple. For most vegetables all you need to do is heat them up by steaming, boiling or microwaving, then add a bit of margarine and butter along with a sprinkle of salt and pepper. For me this formula is especially true with the squash family. The more you try to doctor up a squash the less I like it. A case in point is the acorn squash. It doesn't need all of those fancy marshmallows or a shot of cinnamon or any of that. It is best left adorned by a few simple ingredients.

Women too are best left unadorned — no, I don't mean completely unadorned. That has its advantages, but this is not the time and place. What I mean is that women are best when they aren't doctored up with an excessive amount of makeup. I have noticed that the degree of a woman's confidence varies in inverse proportion to the amount of makeup she wears. It is also a sign that she is happy with herself, and not inclined to put on a false personality for the benefit of the world, (while an entirely different creature exists inside). Marry a girl with a load of makeup and you don't know what you are getting into until after the honeymoon.

Of course, this rule is not a hard and fast one. Spinach can use some adornment and is probably better for being included in a quiche or a salad. Lettuce is good tossed with a bunch of other ingredients. But squash, well, try the following recipe and you will see what I mean.

By the way, when you meet up with a female of the species, don't mention the vegetable theory, even if it compliments her. Women generally take offense at being compared to an acorn squash.

Acorn Squash

Serving Size: 4
Preparation Time: 10 minutes
Ingredients:
1 acorn squash
4 tablespoons margarine or butter
1 dash salt
1 dash pepper

Cut acorn squash in half, length-wise. Scrape out seeds with a spoon. No need to peel. Cut each half in half again. This, of course, means the squash is now in quarters.

Add a pad of butter to the hollowed-out side of each quarter. Sprinkle on salt and pepper. Place on baking dish and put in 375° oven for about an hour.

Eat by scraping soft squash from rind.

Canned vs. Frozen

There are advantages to both frozen and canned vegetables. Generally frozen vegetables retain more vitamins and seem to taste fresher, whereas canned vegetables will sit longer and do not need to be kept constantly frozen. I would also argue that there are times when the taste of a canned vegetable is preferable to the fresher frozen taste. The obvious case is in green bean casserole. I personally like the taste of the leftover juice in canned corn, and you certainly could not make peas-on-brea' with anything but canned peas.

"Peas-on-brea'?" you ask. "I've never heard of that. Is that anything like cordon bleu?"

Actually, you probably have never heard of peas-on-brea' because, as near as I can figure, my family members are the only people who eat this concoction. I think it was developed by of one of my rustic forebears, who was awfully hungry for a large meal but had only a few basic ingredients lying around. It is basically peas with the canned juice, on bread. My sister coined the Frenchified name, for obvious reasons.

It is actually quite tasty, and when my family gets together from disparate parts of the country, peas-on-brea' is one of the delicacies in which we indulge—much to the disgust of the assorted in-laws.

Peas-on-Brea'

Serving Size: 4
Preparation Time: 5 minutes
Ingredients:
1 can peas
2 tablespoons margarine or butter
4 slices bread
1 dash salt
1 dash pepper

Heat peas with their juice in saucepan over medium-high heat or even high if you keep a relatively constant eye on it.

While peas are cooking, evenly spread approximately one-half tablespoon of margarine or butter on one side of the bread. Flop each slice of bread—buttered side up—on a plate.

When peas come to a boil remove from heat. Spread peas on each piece of bread and dump juice over bread making sure to soak the outer crust.

Sprinkle with salt and pepper. Eat immediately; this dish is best when hot.

Salads

In this country we typically eat salad before the meal. For some reason, I never think of salad as part of a meal because it never seems to make a dent in my hunger. I could eat salad all day long and — though my stomach would be bloated and my digestive track loaded clear to the esophagus, I would still be hungry. Salad tastes good. There are times I even crave it, but it just is not filling. A man would not come in from a hard day's work at the mill to eat a few bites of salad in preparation for a pick-up game of basketball at the Y. No, there must be more.

Yet its insubstantial nature does not keep salad from becoming one of the more necessary parts of a person's diet. Salad carries loads of vitamins and essential roughage. Properly doctored lettuce leaves can even be made to taste good. There are many and various types of dressings. My personal favorites are creamy Italian, ranch and Caesar (without the anchovies). A typical salad to complement a meal can be thrown together quite easily. Try the following recipe:

Vegetable Salad

Serving Size: 1
Preparation Time: 20 minutes
Ingredients:
1 head lettuce
1 carrot
2 mushrooms
2 slices ham
4 slices cheddar cheese

You may either cut the lettuce into inch-sized strips using a big knife, or you may rip it to shreds using your bare hands. After a hard day at the office or on the plant floor, I recommend the hands-on method.

Peel and slice carrot as thinly as possible. Some people would shred the carrot, but I think it is too much trouble to clean the shredder. Wash and slice mushrooms. Make ham into cubes or any other cut shapes that also happen to be bite sized. Slice cheese in a similar manner.

Add all ingredients and toss. This does not mean to heave the dish at the nearest, convenient feminist. Rather, mix the ingredients by flipping them around in the bowl.

Add dressing of your choice.

Cucumber Salad

If you are trying to add a bit of "panache" to a meal, a salad is ideal. Remember, substance is not required to make a meal seem high-toned. It is the variety and number of courses that count. That is precisely why salad can be such a handy dish when company is served. It allows you to put another bowl on the table without worrying that the extra food is going to dampen anyone's appetite for the real food that will soon be coming along in the form of the entree.

Of course, there are leafy salads like the one described above, but there are also salads appropriate to other occasions. Summertime calls for cucumber salad. Some would argue that there are other salads more associated with summer. Sure potato salad and fruit salad conjure up images of fried chicken at the park by the beach with sand gritting your teeth. However, there is nothing like a good cucumber salad to whet the appetite just before you flop into a hammock with a beer in one hand and a transistor radio playing a ball game in the other and a plate of steak fresh from the grill balanced on your stomach.

Cucumber Salad

Serving Size: 6
Preparation Time: 10 minutes
Ingredients:
1 or 2 cucumbers
8 ounces sour cream
1 dash pepper

Peel or don't peel cucumbers, depending on your taste — you might try half-peeling them. By this I mean cut off three or four strips of skin slicing lengthwise. However, this looks elegant and a bit fetishistic. I prefer my cukes completely peeled. Cucumber skin can taste bitter.

Slice cucumbers cross-wise. Toss into bowl with sour cream. Add pepper to taste. Mix ingredients.

For a cucumber salad with a zing, throw in some onion slices. When fresh, most of the onion flavor will be concentrated in the onion, but if you let it sit overnight, the onion flavor will spread to the sour cream sauce.

The Skin Controversy

In food preparation there are many controversies. Yet the controversy that seems to divide the population randomly — without reference to gender, creed or economic status — into two equal halves is whether or not skins should be peeled from potatoes used in making potato salad.

I happen to be a partisan who advocates keeping the skins on the potatoes. Although it is true that most of the vitamins of any vegetable are in the skin, who cares? The important thing to me is that potato skins add much needed texture. Without the skins, potato salad is nothing better than mush. You may as well mix up a bowl of gruel. To those of you who do not like potato skins, "Get over it!"

Unfortunately, most stores, restaurants and delis are a slave to their customer base. They know that even people who like skins on their potatoes will eat it without skins. It is the other half of society that is intolerant and will seldom place a tentative toe across the boundary of true adventure. They would rather stay in their safe shell of pabulum and skinlessness. In order for us venturesome types to get our quota of potato salad with the skin on, we must make it ourselves.

Potato Salad

Serving Size: 16
Preparation Time: 1 hour
Ingredients:
8 potatoes
6 eggs—hard-boiled
4 or 5 heaping tablespoons mayonnaise
1 onion
1 tablespoon mustard
3 dashes paprika
1 dash salt
3 dashes pepper

Put eggs in water in saucepan to hard-boil. Clean potatoes, cube in about ½-inch chunks and boil until soft. (I like to leave the potatoes unpeeled.) Dice the onion. Shell the eggs and cut into small pieces. Throw these ingredients into a LARGE bowl, along with salt and pepper, mayo and mustard. Mix thoroughly. You may have to do this with your hands to do a proper job of it. Don't worry about smashing the potatoes. Some would say that smashing makes for an even better potato salad.

Smooth the mixture in bowl so that the top is flat. Sprinkle on the paprika in a tic-tac-toe pattern. Make sure the Xs win. You'll look foolish if you let the Os win. (When the Os win, it's a sign you really don't know how to play the game.)

Place mixture in refrigerator for a few hours to let the onion flavor spread through the salad and also to let them soften somewhat.

You can also try adding chopped pickles for a different flavor, or chopped peppers for an added crunch.

Suggested Beer: Papst Blue Ribbon.

Serving Ideas: Best with ham and baked beans or a juicy steak just off the grill.

Tomatoes

Believe it or not, there are people who do not like fresh tomatoes. I did not know this was possible until my wife divulged to me her secret. I was appalled. Our marriage went through a deep crisis. Until this revelation I had thought of us as a compatible duo, with similar likes and dislikes. As long as she let me exercise my bad sense of humor and drone on about politics, we got along. Suddenly a great shadow had arisen between us. How could the woman I love be so cold and callous as not to share my deep desire for tomatoes?

It was not until we moved to the Seattle area that this problem between us was resolved. You see, every year I plant a few tomato plants. In the Northwest tomato plants have a tendency to get blighted and yield a small amount of produce. Now, with minuscule crops, I found myself not wanting to share the meager produce available. I now huddle protectively over my tomatoes like a dog over his bone. The great Northwest has made me thankful my wife does not like tomatoes . . . all the more for me.

Tomatoes have many uses beyond their roll in a salad. They are used in all kinds of processed food from salsa to spaghetti sauce. They can even be dried to good effect and put in sauces and soups. They are great plain with a shaker of salt or sliced and laid out on a plate.

I usually consume tomatoes in two ways. First, I have a passion for tomato sandwiches. Second, I love tomato and cottage cheese salad. I know, I know. It doesn't sound appetizing; kind of like peanut butter and banana sandwiches, or corn in a marinara sauce. Yet I have found myself looking forward more and more every year to tomato season simply so I can indulge myself in this one dish.

Tomato and Cottage Cheese Salad

Serving Size: 4
Preparation Time: 10 minutes
Ingredients:
4 tomatoes
12 ounces cottage cheese
4 teaspoons chives
1 dash salt
1 dash pepper

Cut the stem and the place it attaches from the tomatoes. Then, slicing downward but making sure not to cut all the way through, slice each tomato into eighths. The effect should be that of a flower.

Plop a spoonful of cottage cheese in the center of each tomato. Sprinkle on spices and pile the chives into the center of the cottage cheese.

Taco Salad

The strange thing about recipes that have their roots in Mexico is that they all have pretty much the same ingredients—you know, corn chips, refried beans, hamburger, taco seasoning and lettuce. The basic difference in the recipes lies primarily in mode of preparation and in relative quantities of each ingredient. Alas, my recipe for taco salad is no different. It, indeed, contains all the ingredients enumerated above plus a few more. However, it does possess the advantage of being versatile and allows each individual consuming the dish to concoct a plate that will be geared specifically to his own taste.

This makes the cook's job sound easy. Unfortunately, this is not the case. I find that taco salad is one of the more laborious dishes to make. One must chop up innumerable vegetables placed in several dishes, fry the hamburger in one pan, while heating the refried beans in another. This recipe is a solid hour of work. Yet in the end the chef is rewarded by eager faces and rounded bellies. He also has the option of indulging in a bean fetish that is not always permitted under normal circumstances. Finger pulling will be a much favored sport after this meal is concluded.

Taco Salad

Servings: 4
Preparation Time: 25 minutes
Ingredients:
1 pound hamburger
1 onion
1 carrot
4 mushrooms
1 packet of taco seasoning
1 head lettuce
1 tomato
4 tablespoons salsa
4 tablespoons sour cream
1 bag corn chips

Slice and dice the onion carrot and mushrooms. Fry hamburger in skillet. Drain off fat from burger. Add in taco seasoning and water as per instructions on taco seasoning packet.

While letting the hamburger cook down, slice lettuce and tomato. On each serving plate, lay down a bed of corn chips, layer on lettuce and tomatoes along with the hamburger concoction. Finally, top with sour cream and salsa.

For extra flavor and heaviness throw some grated cheese (cheddar) on the burger just before the sour cream.

Soups and Sandwiches

Soups

Soup can be used to start a meal in the same way you would serve a leafy salad. Although multiple course meals are more trouble than they may be worth, there will be times when such extravagance will be warranted, to placate a loved-one for not remembering her birthday, or for refusing to take a walk on a crisp fall Sunday afternoon because the football season has started.

The only problem with soups as the first course is that, unlike salads, they tend to be substantial, and they quickly fill a gaping maw as well as the huge pit behind. If you insist on serving soup before a meal, do it in small quantities or be faced with guests eating insufficient quantities of the main dish. You do not want to be left with huge quantities of leftovers. Besides, as any cook will tell you, the prime satisfaction in making a meal is seeing your guests wolf down the main course, and subsequently being incapable of suppressing a loud belch. (That's another reason I usually serve beer instead of wine to guests.)

Soup is best as the main course of a simple meal, especially during basketball season when a sit-down meal at the table is an imposition and the only company you really want are a few guys from the office who care more about the final four than they do about being offered a finger bowl. Dipping a cup in a huge pan of soup is the most efficient way to serve and be served during a twenty-second time-out. Just don't forget to set the crackers on the coffee table. Such an error might result in an untimely dash to the kitchen. You are likely to miss a perfect three pointer from the top of the key that will decide the game. Sure, they will show it in replay, but you can't say you really saw it if you don't see it as it happens. Anyone can watch a replay. To truly understand a great play, one must have viewed it in the context of the game as it occurs, not as an isolated incident. I don't know why women can't understand this subtlety. My wife always insists that I look at her when she speaks to me during a game. She thinks that I don't hear what she is saying until she sees my eyes focused upon her. Little does she know that I have mastered the art of seeming to listen—and it really doesn't matter if I am making eye contact or not. Yet, I can't risk making even this gesture on the chance I might miss an important play.

Another advantage of soup is that it does not require a sense of timing. Once it is made, it can set on the stove for hours to be devoured at any time. For those of us who are continuous eaters, this is a great advantage.

Soup can be made from almost anything, although I would not make it from meat loaf, which is already made out of almost anything—the loaf part tends to gum up the works. Thus, making soup is a good way to get rid of leftovers. You can toss nearly any kind of meat into a pot of boiling water along with some onions, sliced potatoes, add some salt and pepper; and in an hour or two you will have a nice pot of soup. A good example of a soup concocted from leftovers is Leftover Chicken Soup:

Leftover Chicken Soup

Serving Size: 4
Preparation Time: 15 minutes
Ingredients:
1 semi-eaten roasted chicken
1 potato
1 carrot
1 onion
1 dash salt
1 dash pepper
1 dash parsley
1 dash basil

Strip the remains of your roast chicken and place whatever meat you may have gathered in a pan. Chop potato carrot and onion and toss in the pan. Put enough water in the pan to just cover ingredients.

Add spices to taste. Cover pan and cook on low or simmer for a few hours, until vegetables are tender.

Broth vs. Cream

As a general rule, meat soups are broth based and vegetable soups are cream based. Ever heard of cream of beef soup? Beef is heavy enough on its own. It is the vegetables which need cream to give them body. Cream of mushroom, cream of tomato and cream of celery are a few common examples. You can find any one of these creamy vegetable soups in a can. All of them make a tolerable lunchtime meal especially if swallowed with a sandwich and a hot cup of coffee. Yet you can add just a few ingredients to a canned soup and make it even better, some spices like garlic or basil, or even some frozen vegetables. Ramen soups are even amenable to this treatment. Try adding a half a cup of frozen peas and carrots to any of the Ramen family of soups. You would be surprised at how it spruces them up.

Speaking of doctoring prepackaged soups: my tomato soup recipe is as good as any soup served in a restaurant. I am convinced that, every day all over the country, tall-hatted chefs stand before huge stainless steel pots cracking open large cans of Campbell's tomato soup. They add some milk and toss in their preferred spices. Is it authentic to prepare a dish this way? Heck no. But the result is delicious—and the ingredients are cheap—so why not?

Tomato Basil Soup

Serving Size: 1
Preparation Time: 15 minutes
Ingredients:
1 can tomato soup—condensed
1½ cups milk
3 dashes pepper
3 dashes parsley
3 dashes basil

In saucepan on medium heat, mix all ingredients until hot. Never cook a milk on high—it will scorch the bottom of the pan and smell like a baby who can't keep his formula down.

Serving Ideas: With crackers or bread and butter.

Thinking about the Future

As you are huddled with a pile of crackers over a bowl of your favorite soup, you can feel the warmth steam through your bones. People have enjoyed soup for centuries. At least they have enjoyed it as long as there has been fire and pots within which to cook a broth.

But what about the future? Will there be soup in the brave new world that approaches? Will there be a brave new world? Some alarmists hypothesize that we are running out of the fuels that we will need to sustain our drive into the next millennium. You ask, "How do we plan to launch space shuttles, power space stations and colonize Mars, let alone take care of the needs of our own planet?" Let me put forth the hypothesis that there is, in reality, no shortage of fuel, for nothing can generate gas and lift people out of their chairs like a bowl or two of bean soup. I have set in the presence of men who could generate enough methane gas to send themselves into orbit. Sometimes I marvel that the earth has not been knocked out of its rotation or at least changed in polarity with the ferociousness of their expostulations. The legitimate question is not *if* there will be energy, but *how* to harness the energy we already know exists. I think something like a system of suction cups hooked up to a vacuum device similar to those used on milk cows would suffice. However, I shall leave it to the scientists and engineers to deal with the details.

Carrying this discussion further than anyone other than myself might wish to venture, I must point out that there are differences among fuels created by various beans. Lima bean soup, for example, is known to create a loud poof that—like a magician's wand—can make people vanish. Though plentiful, lima bean gas does not make the best fuel. Unfortunately, it is too light—although it does flash well in a burning chamber.

Then there is navy bean soup, a generator of a continuous barrage of minor putts, not unlike a motorboat running at idle speed. This will likely make the best rocket fuel as it can be more reliably harnessed. It is also a heavy fuel. Its only drawback is that it leaves a green contrail.

For domestic uses, black bean soup would answer best. It creates a delicate but irrepressible sound that is accompanied by the same fleuro-carbons once used as a propellant in WD-40. Suffice it to say that this will peel the rust from any stuck bolt.

There are other varieties too. All possess tremendous potential. Unfortunately, in our unenlightened age, the end result of any bean soup is generally underutilized. Instead of propelling the world into the future, when you break out the bean soup, your wife refuses to watch TV with you, taking up reading murder mysteries instead. And the kids lock themselves in their room, willingly attacking their homework, because it is preferable to being in your presence.

Finally, on the nutritional level, beans contain plenty of protein and therefore are used by vegetarians as a substitute for meat. Besides all its other advantages, bean soup just plain tastes good.

Lima Bean Soup

Serving Size: 6
Preparation Time: 20 minutes
Ingredients:
¾ cup lima beans
3 cups water
1 carrot
1 potato
2 slices ham
½ tablespoon parsley
¼ tablespoon basil
1 dash rosemary
3 dashes pepper
1 onion

Put beans in saucepan. Cut up vegetables and ham. Add all, including spices to pan. Set heat on high. Bring to boil then set at simmer and cover. Cook for about 3 hours.

This soup will provide locomotion when all other fuels fail.

Potato: The All-American Vegetable

Of all the soup recipes I have concocted, the one that seems to be most popular is potato soup. It may just be that the potato is the all-American vegetable. People think the Irish were dependent on the potato before the famous potato famine of the late 1840s. We make so many things out of potatoes. Imagine if we had a blight. No French fries with your burgers. No mashed spuds with your fried chicken. No baked potato with your steak. Of course people wouldn't starve to death the way they did in Ireland, but there sure would be a lot of grumpy folks running around.

A few friends and I sat around one day and tried to think of all the ways a potato can be cooked. It was an intellectual exercise from which I have not yet recovered. Some folks like to go to art museums and try to contort the chaos on canvas into some intelligible form in their head. I would rather make productive use of my time.

Of course, potatoes may be baked. They can be boiled, fried with onions, French-fried, mashed and curly fried. They are made into potato chips, and potato skins are baked with cheese. I could go on for the possibilities are endless. Yet, the only way that I have never seen anyone eat a potato is in its raw state. So for research purposes I tried a raw potato. It did not take me long to figure out why most people cook them.

Since you have to cook them to enjoy them anyway, try cooking up a pot of potato soup.

Potato Soup

Serving Size: 8
Preparation Time: 15 minutes
Ingredients:
8 potatoes—cut in cubes
1 onion—cut in cubes
4 mushrooms—cut in strips
1 quart milk
1 dash pepper
1 tablespoon parsley
1 teaspoon basil
2 teaspoons butter

Cut up potatoes, onions and mushrooms. Boil until potatoes are soft. Dump excess water. Add milk, butter and spices. Cook for an additional five minutes or so.

Chile, Chilly, Chili

Why so many spellings and meanings for the same word? Are they related? Does a person eat chili when they are chilly? Or is Chile a cool place where they grow chili peppers? I suppose having asked these important questions I should provide some answers. Yes, it can get chilly in Chile and chili will warm you up. Also, the rain in Spain stays mainly in the plain.

If there is one soup considered to be within the province of the male of the species it is indeed chili. Chili requires a strong hand, a strong stomach and a passionate disregard for one's own safety. You would not normally see a woman crushing a beer can on her skull. Similarly, she is very reticent about tossing a handful of dried peppercorns into a flaming brew with a batch of kidney beans and hamburger. This is why such bravado is left to us men who can perform such deeds with reckless abandon and disregard for consequences.

There are two requirements for chili: It must burn the mouth, even if consumed cold, and it must drain the nasal cavities even in the midst of a severe head cold. Anything that does not fulfill these requirements is mere pap.

Chili, made and eaten correctly, is an experience, sublime, ephemeral and mystical. It should transport the eater to another plane beyond which transcendental meditation can only hint. Buddhist monks sit for hours chanting their mantras and cannot even get close to the place where a simple bowl of chili could bring them.

A perfect bowl of chili in conjunction with a stack of saltines will irresistibly crease the human face with a broad grin. The first bite will elevate the adenoids and lower the diaphragm, and thus send the mind outside of the realm of normal body senses, for suddenly, the entire being is focused on the tongue. Being thus focused is the end desire of all human endeavors. With a good bowl of chili you will see there is no longer a need to pursue, wealth, women and lowboy Harleys. Okay, there may still be a reason to desire a Harley, and money can be useful. As for women, what would we do without them? Still, a good bowl of chili will make you forget all that, if only for the instant that it sets the tongue on fire and blazes a burning trail down the throat.

For the proper chili experience, don't forget the saltine crackers and a cold beer as a chaser.

Chili

Serving Size: 8
Preparation Time: 25 minutes
Ingredients:
1 pound hamburger
1 onion—cut in cubes
4 mushrooms—cut in strips
1 24-ounce can of red kidney beans
6 cups V8
1 tablespoon parsley
1 teaspoon red pepper
½ teaspoon chili powder
1 tablespoon crushed red peppers
1 dash black pepper—to taste

Fry up burger and onions in the bottom of a stew pot. When the burger is browned, drain off the fat and dump in the remaining ingredients. Bring mixture to a boil, then turn down to simmer for at least an hour—this to extract as much flavor as possible from the peppers. You may want to vary the peppers to suit your own tastes.

Suggested Beer: Cold and from a brown bottle.

Onion Soup

Around the world there are many rituals for a young man just entering manhood. It has been established in most societies that at coming of age a young man must be tested to determine if he is brave. Men need to know that their fellows will have the courage to stand with them in time of danger or battle. This ceremony also makes a young man aware that he is a part of something far greater than himself, a band of brothers, a natural and exclusive society dedicated to protecting hearth, home and country, a club devoted most of all to the idea that it is our inalienable right to watch football (or its equivalent in other nations) on Sunday afternoons without being asked to go shopping or to take out the recycle bins.

Manhood in some cultures is attained by dint of a sexual coming of age. It is attained in others by a bout with a bottle of vodka and a whirling polka. (The combination of which is likely to produce extreme queasiness.) The Jewish culture, I believe, has the one requiring the most courage. However, I will refrain from discussing it on the grounds that every time I think about it, I wince. In America, the melting pot of the world, a formal ceremony for induction into manhood has somehow fallen into disuse. Yet below the surface of our enlightened society the test still lingers and is imposed upon our youth in the form of . . . the ONION.

Indeed, wherever young men gather the ritual continues. I can still remember my friends saying, "Hey, a real man can eat an entire onion raw!" I must confess to a love of onions, yet at my own coming of age I was daunted by the idea. I am proud to say that I became a man at ten years of age after a medium-sized Vedalia onion, two cans of Coca-Cola and a bellyache.

Luckily, French onion soup does not require the consumption of whole raw onions. It does, though, require quite a number of cooked ones.

French Onion Soup

Serving Size: 4
Preparation Time: 25 minutes
Ingredients:
1 can beef broth
1½ cups water
5 onions
4 slices Swiss cheese
4 slices toast
2 tablespoons margarine

Put margarine in a frying pan and cook at a medium heat until it gets good and hot. Add onions that have been sliced into quarter-inch thick ringlets. No need to separate them, they will do so of their own accord when they are frequently stirred by you to keep them from sticking to the bottom of the pan.

When the onions have softened up, you can move them to a big soup pan. Add water and beef broth. Let stew on a low heat setting for as long as you like.

When you are ready to serve, toss a piece of toast into a bowl. Put a piece of cheese on top of that, and ladle soup over all of that.

Lunchtime

Say "cheese!" Yes, the favorite food of mice is also one of the favorites of men. Cheese comes in a variety of flavors: cheddar, American, Swiss, Gorgonzola, mozzarella, etc. It is one of those ubiquitous ingredients that will complement nearly any dish and even tastes good on its own.

Cheese for men is like chocolate for women. We can eat it any time, anywhere, on anything and it is also a kind of aphrodisiac. Chocolate is reported to spawn endorphins in a woman's brain causing them to want to go to bed. This is why men have forever given women candy for almost any occasion.

Cheese makes a man feel like he has actually eaten something. Since mankind has only a few primal urges to which he pays any attention, when hunger is gone, there is only one left . . . the urge to go to bed. More often than not, this leads to a prolonged nap to recover from a session at the table, but on occasion it also has other desired effects.

There are not too many hard and fast rules about cheese. The main one to remember is that marinara sauces normally take mozzarella, ricotta or

Parmesan. Otherwise, you can mix and match to your heart's content. However, most cheese soups use yellow cheese. If you want to get your fill of cheese in a dish that also contains every man's favorite vegetable, try out this recipe. Top it off with a nap and you will have the perfect lunchtime meal.

Cheese and Broccoli Soup with a Baked Potato

Serving Size: 4
Preparation Time: 15 minutes
Ingredients:
4 potatoes
1 can cheese soup
1 can of milk
½ head broccoli
1 dash pepper
1 dash garlic powder

Potatoes may be baked in the oven, in which case they should be wrapped in foil and baked at 375° for about an hour. Or they may be cooked in the microwave for about ten minutes after having been thoroughly punctured with a fork.

While potatoes are cooking, place cheese soup (you can also use cheese and broccoli soup) in a sauce pan, add 1 can of milk. Set on medium heat. Cut broccoli into fairly small pieces—if you are willing to cook this for a while you can put the broccoli directly into the soup. However, if you are in a hurry, you might wish to blast them with the microwave for about three minutes first.

Add spices to soup. When soup and potatoes are both done, slice into potato top and place in a bowl. Dump soup over potato. You can also sprinkle a few chopped chives on top of this for a classy look, or even some bacon bits.

To make this recipe really easy, use broccoli cheese soup instead of muddling around with fresh broccoli.

Sandwiches

Most people know the story about how the Earl of Sandwich invented the concept of putting meat and other ingredients between two slices of bread. He was so addicted to playing cards that he refused to be called away from the gaming table to eat a regular meal. What many people don't know is that the good Earl also invented the catheter for the same reason.

The concept and execution of sandwiches is quite simple, and there is not a man on the North American continent who could not create a master-piece of the art form with a well-stocked refrigerator and a jar of Miracle Whip. Therefore, I shall not try to instruct where there is no need. There is, however, a type of sandwich I discovered during my days in the Navy, while doing a short port visit in Toulon, France.

It seemed that on every street corner there was a kiosk dedicated to making something they called the "American Sandwich." I am sure that the vendors changed the name of the sandwich to whichever nationality had a ship in port. We called them "French Squish Sandwiches." An appellation you will under-stand when you read this recipe.

French Squish Sandwich

Serving Size: 4
Preparation Time: 20 minutes
Ingredients:
4 hoagie buns
1 pound hamburger
1 tomato
4 leaves lettuce
1 package French fries
1 dash salt
1 dash pepper

Prepare fries according to package directions. Form elongated squares geared to fit on hoagie buns. Fry or grill burger, sprinkling on salt and pepper. Slice tomato.

Warm up your waffle grill.

When hamburger and French fries are cooked, lay hamburger between bun topped by fries—yes, I said fries—and tomato and lettuce. When waffle grill is warm, squish sandwich. This is an essential part of the process because it warms the bun and keeps the fries from falling out.

Dips and Your Friends

If you are lucky enough to have friends who drop by unannounced, then you have also been put in a situation where you have nothing to eat because friends who don't call first are the same people who raid the refrigerator without asking. They will consume your beer, eat your leftover roast beast and slop down the cottage cheese. They will dirty all the dishes and when they see you have nothing left to bother with, they will go home and leave you to clean up the mess.

Fortunately for you, these people are not willing to go through the trouble of preparing any food. This means that you will at least have a bag of blue corn chips that miraculously got overlooked and a few cans in the cupboard. This will be adequate to throw together a little something to munch on while you consummate your date with the remote control and three channels of ESPN.

Bean dip. Yes, bean dip is what you want. It tastes great even with the blue corn chips, and if your buddy returns to make sure he did not miss anything, you can claim it is a bean paste that your dermatologist prescribed to keep your pores dry. Just hope that he doesn't ask you to demonstrate.

Bean Dip

Serving Size: 8
Preparation Time: 15 minutes
Ingredients:
1 can refried beans
10 ounces salsa
3 dashes chili powder
3 dashes pepper
1 dash paprika

In a saucepan over medium heat, dump can of beans. Add salsa and spices. Cook until it bubbles. You will want to keep an eye on this stuff and stir regularly otherwise you may end up burning the bottom.

You can also spruce this recipe up a bit by adding onions and chili peppers. However, if you do this, you should let the concoction set in the refrigerator for a day or so, so that the flavor of the onions, etc., has a chance to permeate the dip.

I normally eat the dip hot, but it is equally good cold.

Pasta and Starches

Starches: Not Just for Pressing Shirts Anymore

So, you have seen the big announcement. Starches have branched out and become their own food group, They are wedged somewhere between the grains and vegetables on the new food pyramid. In the same way that armies need privates (cannon fodder), the same way hives need worker bees (everyone knows the drones do the real work though), as pillows require feathers, starches are those staple-filler foods that no meal can do without. Their roll call may seem bland and flavorless: potatoes, rice, pasta, etc. Yet they make a meal filling, provide it with nutrients and energy and are the greatest receptacle devised by man or nature for the wonders of the culinary arts.

When you plan out a meal, you should do so with the intention of including items from three areas: meat, vegetable, and — of course — starch. If any one of these items is missing, the meal seems incomplete, unfulfilling.

Indeed, there is something spiritual about bulking up on potatoes. Many philosophic movements were begun by people who did not have enough rice or pasta in their diet. Take the Cynics for example. "Cynic" is Greek for dog, with very good reason; it was the Cynics who developed the notion that a man should live like a dog, including his diet. It is a well-known fact that Plato developed his ideal "Platonic" reality because he hadn't gotten his quota of pasta salad and was feeling a bit peaked. All he could think about was the perfect twirly noodle. Even in modern times, existentialism was the outgrowth of food rationing brought on by the struggle of two world wars. Camus couldn't seem to get any wild rice to go with his duck l'orange. You see what a chaotic mess has been brought about by a search for substance in the human diet?

To prevent the possibility of the rise of another impossible-to-comprehend philosophical movement, try Oven-Fried Potatoes with almost anything. It is great especially with Chicken Gorgonzola.

Oven-Fried Potatoes

Serving Size: 6
Preparation Time: 15 minutes
Ingredients:
6 potatoes
1 tablespoon parsley
1 tablespoon basil
1 dash garlic powder
1 dash pepper
2 tablespoons oil

Spread oil in a 13×9-inch baking dish.
Clean and cut potatoes into bite-sized chunks. Toss potatoes in pan and sprinkle on spices. Put in oven at 375° for about an hour, possibly an hour and a half. Start these bad boys early because you are never quite sure how long it will take for them to become

edible. I like to leave mine bake long enough for the outside to become crunchy and the inside to become soft.

This is one of those dishes that it is hard to screw up unless you forget to check on it once in a while.

Stealing Recipes

Potatoes O'Diana is one of those recipes where I feel compelled to give credit to someone else. As much as I find the idea distasteful, intellectual honesty forces me to act. I borrowed this recipe from my sister-in-law. I'm not sure where she got it, but suffice it to say that it originated somewhere in the great Midwest.

This recipe brings up a huge moral dilemma. Who owns a recipe and what constitutes a copyright or patent infringement? I admittedly quite freely borrow from the culinary expertise of others. I do not hesitate to ask someone how they made a dish and then write it up as my own; though only after I have tried it out and tweaked it. Yet, I will make attributions to the creator of a recipe if that creator can indeed be found.

Recipes are a lot like jokes. They circulate and no one can pin down their origin, and each retelling seems to bring with it its own modifications. Legally, you can borrow any idea. What you CANNOT borrow is the exact language of a recipe. That, like any other written document, is owned by the author. Nevertheless, we real men attempt to give credit where credit is due; while at the same time we only secretly crave the accolades of others. Thus, you may feel free to copy recipes from this book word-for-word and claim them for your own, UNLESS you plan to reproduce them for profit. (If that is the case, please tell me how you made your bundle and remit a share to yours truly.)

Enough of this pseudo-legalese. I suggest you try out my sister-in-law's recipe. . . .

Potatoes O'Diana

Serving Size: 8
Preparation Time: 15 minutes
Ingredients:
1 32-ounce bag of frozen hash-brown potatoes
8 ounces sour cream
1 onion
2 ounces cheddar cheese—shredded
1 can cream of mushroom soup
½ stick butter or margarine

Spread out potatoes in a 9×13-inch baking pan. Since the hash browns are frozen, there may be some big chunks stuck together. Break these up while they are still in the bag. However, don't get carried away. I have slammed a bag down on the floor with a throw that "The Body" Ventura would have envied. Yes, the potatoes were broken up as intended, but they were also scattered all over the kitchen, which was not intended.

Melt the butter or margarine, and spread it over the frozen potatoes. Slice and chop the onion. Spread it over the potatoes as well. Now, in a separate bowl (I hate this "separate bowl" business—it just makes for more cleanup—unfortunately, in this case, it is necessary.) mix the mushroom soup, the sour cream and most of the cheese. Ladle this onto the top of the potatoes and spread as evenly as possible.

Finally, sprinkle on the cheese you have left and stick pan into a 400-or-so-degree oven for an hour, perhaps longer depending on if you like crunchy, browned or blackened bits of potatoes.

The Importance of Bacon

In salads, on potatoes, in spaghetti sauce, bacon can show up anywhere. That swelling smoky aroma that fills the lungs and turns the mouth into a cascading waterfall of saliva lends a flavor you cannot beat.

When you are at a loss for a way to spruce up a dish, the solution may be as simple as that skinny bottle in the fridge. Add it to chili or vegetables, or even put it between two slices of bread. You can add it to almost any dish with a degree of impunity equaled only by pepper and salt.

A cautionary note: Do NOT buy imitation bacon. It's a bit like buying imitation food. Sure, you can put it in your mouth and swallow it, but can you taste it or digest it? Stick with the real thing.

For those with religious scruples regarding bacon, there is no replacement. A lack of bacon is the sacrifice you make for your beliefs. Indeed, there is no such thing as kosher bacon. I have often wondered whom I should admire more for their ability to self-sacrifice: the Orthodox Jew or the Catholic priest. After all, the priest's abstinence only seems unbearable the first seventy or eighty years of his existence; but it would be nigh on impossible to forgo bacon till Kingdom-Come, whether you were waiting for the first coming or the second.

Bacon-Wrapped Baked Potato

Serving Size: 8
Preparation Time: 15 minutes
Ingredients:
8 potatoes
8 slices bacon

Thoroughly wash potatoes. Remove eyes by scratching them out with your thumbnail. Tear off eight strips of aluminum foil wide enough to completely wrap a potato.

Wrap bacon slice around each potato. Place potato on foil. Pick up the four corners of the foil and bring them together. Then twist so that the potato is snug in the foil but seam is on top. This is important if you wish to keep the bacon grease from dripping onto the base of the oven.

Place potatoes in oven at about 375°. Cook for 1 to 1½ hours. You may puncture a potato with a fork to check for doneness. Just be careful where you poke it.

Pizza Toppings

When ordering a pizza, the average person weighs the cost of multiple pizza toppings with the relative benefit to the palate. It is a difficult decision because it is not easy to quantify the taste of baked mushrooms. Is it worth a dollar fifty to taste that soft-crunch that comes from a green pepper? Is it worth the extra cash to experience the aftertaste that comes from a black olive?

If you are like me, when you order out, you are likely to end up with a cheese pizza.

However, a home-baked pizza does not carry with it this stark choice. Instead, a person is faced merely with the pleasant contemplation of what combination of toppings will best quell those rumblings currently creating chaos in the stomach.

Different combinations appeal to different appetites. My personal favorite combination is the standard fare of pepperoni, mushrooms and onions, with marinara sauce laced with red pepper and garlic. I like to think that this succinctly reflects my personality. Strong, warm-blooded, sometimes introverted and very often possessed of garlic breath.

Psychologists should take note. If you really want to understand your clientele, offer to buy them pizza with unlimited toppings. Those who require ham and pineapple are in need of a Hawaiian vacation. Those who like sausage and multiple meat toppings have sublimated their animal urgings. A person who must have strictly vegetarian toppings is obviously in need of a little loosening up, they take the world too seriously.

Watch out for the fellow who has cravings for diced squid or imagines his mother has something to do with his primal longing for cantaloupe. Worse yet is the guy who says he will just have cheese. He's likely to stiff you when it comes time to pay the therapy bill.

The Standard Pizza

Serving Size: 8
Preparation Time: 20 minutes
Ingredients:
1 box Jiffy pizza dough
5 tablespoons flour
½ cup from a can of Hunt's sausage spaghetti sauce
½ onion
12 ounces pepperoni—sliced
5 fresh mushrooms
8 ounces shredded mozzarella cheese
1½ tablespoons olive oil
1 dash pepper
1 dash red pepper

Mix boxed dough with flour and add just enough warm tap water to dampen all dry ingredients. (This isn't much water, so go light on the water and only add more if the dough seems crumbly.) This makes a light and crispy, yet thick crust.

Spread 1 tablespoon of olive oil evenly over pizza pan. Now plop the pizza dough onto the pan. Make a well in the dough (it will be sticky). Dump in remaining oil and spread in a circular motion until crust reaches the outer edges of the pan.

Pop into oven at 425° for about 10 minutes. While this is baking, take the opportunity to chop onions, mushrooms, etc.

When the required 10 minutes to cook the crust have elapsed, remove it from the oven, spread on sauce, sprinkle on spices and toss on the remaining toppings—making sure to leave the cheese for last.

Put back in oven and cook for 12 to 16 minutes.

You may experiment with toppings and sauces to make your own optimum pizza.

No. 13

I used to think that macaroni was macaroni, and pasta was pasta. In a strictly physical sense this is true. Even though most pastas are made of the same ingredients, there is indeed a difference in taste generated by the various shapes.

There are also differences in sauce retention. For example a spaghetti will not hold marinara sauce in the same way a shell will hold it. Twirly noodles are great with white sauces and can take the place of egg noodles in many dishes.

When picking a pasta, it is best to understand your objective. A thin sauce requires a more contoured noodle: pinwheels, elbow macaroni or shells. For thick sauces flat noodles are permissible: spaghetti and linguini. Even these, though, can differ in size and effect. Making a dish with the wrong noodle can be like trying to play baseball with a football. A football won't fly very far when hit by a baseball bat. By the same token, macaroni doesn't fly very far in a clam sauce.

Some pastas are numbered by their size. Linguini sizes are especially important. There are numbers 12, 13 and 14. No. 13 is the optimum size. 12 is insufficient in width to hold an adequate amount of sauce and 14 is too thick. No. 13 is not generally considered a lucky number. Builders have been known to leave the number off from elevator buttons. Yet for linguini it is the best possible pasta.

Many pasta packages mention "al dente." This is the transcendental state of cooked pasta, above dried and below soggy. In Italian "dente" means dentures and graphically depicts what you will need if you eat the pasta before it is cooked to this level.

There is one final rule: in the end pasta is indeed pasta. If you run out of the optimum pasta, just toss in a different one. It will still work—perhaps not as well, but it will work. You see, you *can* play baseball with a football. It will just make the game a little more physical—and sometimes even more fun.

Linguini

Serving Size: 8
Preparation Time: 20 minutes
Ingredients:
1 jar Four Brother's Creamy Pesto
1 chopped onion
4 fresh mushrooms—sliced
1 dash pepper
2 tablespoons Parmesan cheese
1 dash parsley
1 dash basil
1 tablespoon olive oil
1 pound No. 13 linguini

Place big pot of water on stove on high.

In separate saucepan spread olive oil over bottom and turn burner to medium heat. Add onions and mushrooms. Fry for about 3 minutes, until somewhat tender. Dump in sauce and spices and Parmesan cheese. Turn burner to simmer.

Meanwhile, your pot of boiling water should have had a chance to come to a boil. Now break linguini in half (unless you like slopping sauce all over your face when you eat). Toss in linguini noodles, making sure that they do not go into the pan all in the same direction. If you have had problems with sticky pasta in the past, try adding some oil to the boiling water (a tablespoon or so). More or less continuously stir the pasta to prevent sticking and ensure even cooking. When pasta seems floppy, bite into a piece to test its *al dente*ness. When noodles are done to your satisfaction, drain off water and dump pasta onto plates.

Spoon sauce over noodles. Serve immediately.

Serving Ideas: This dish goes well with a green vegetable or even an orange one (like carrots) — no yellow vegetables, please.

Suggested Beer: Best beer in this case is something fancy with a bouquet, either a Red Wolf or a Killian's Red; baring those, a Pabst will do.

Italian Wines

I am no wine connoisseur, yet I have had some experience with this ubiquitous beverage. This much I can tell you: wines take on some of the character of the place in which they are produced.

I do not know if this is because climate has the same effect on grapes as it does on people. Or if it is because people put some of their personality in a wine when they produce it. I suspect that the answer here is "a little of both."

Thus French wines tend to be snooty and pretentious — with a delicate bouquet. German wines are hearty, robust and have a panzer division waiting to strike the unwary, and American wines are bourgeois knock-offs of the French. Spanish wines are sweet yet surreal and East European wines typically wear a babushka. Now, in my mind, the best wines for all occasions are Italian wines. They tend to have that smiling goodfella feel that lightens a heavy meal and makes a light meal a little more fun.

Italian wine is the only one that comes close to being able to match beer in appropriateness with pizza or Mexican dishes. Nevertheless, no wine, regardless of national origin, is appropriate with any dish during the Superbowl.

Prosciutto al Twirly Noodles

Serving Size: 6
Preparation Time: 20 minutes
Ingredients:
4 slices ham
2 tablespoons margarine
2 tablespoons flour
2 dashes pepper
1 cup milk
1/8 cup Parmesan cheese
1/3 cup peas
1 package pasta

Cut ham slices into small pieces. Toss into frying pan on medium heat. When they have been thoroughly warmed, shove them to the side of the pan. Add margarine. When it has melted, add flower. Make sure that all of the flower is made damp by the margarine. When you have succeeded in this task without burning the contents of the pan, add milk, peas, pepper, cheese. Stir until the contents thicken. This will not take very long.

Now, while you were doing all of this, you should have also been working on boiling some water in a good-sized pan. When the water is boiling, add noodles and stir occasionally until the noodles are done. You can use any kind of noodles that you want, from those twirly ones down to macaroni or penne or even spaghetti. In any case, when the noodles are done, strain (don't grunt when you do this, as it is unbecoming a real man who is not actually performing a strenuous physical task).

Dump strained noodles in with the sauce, and stir.

Suggested Beer: Dos Equiis. I know it's not Italian, but if it tastes right, go with it.

Serving Ideas: This can be one of those stand-alone dishes.

Company Foods

Some dishes simply lend themselves to being served to guests. When I was a kid and my father brought visiting associates home from work, my mom would always fix the same meal, spaghetti. I have done some work for the local shelter and have found that, invariably, the best meal to serve is, spaghetti.

Spaghetti is good for guests because it is easy to make, self-contained, goes well with anything, and most importantly, almost everyone likes it. Lasagna is another such dish. Lasagna is even better because it carries all of the food groups and can be balanced at the peak of the newfangled food pyramid.

When having guests, it is best to stay away from foods that require precise timing or elaborate preparations. The temptation to make Chicken Gorgonzola for a dinner party may be near overwhelming. However, it can result in a gloppy sauce poured over dried-up, cold chicken.

It is best to keep company food simple and plentiful. Besides, if you succeed in pulling off a fancy dish, your friends will end up insulting you by calling you an esthete or an Epicurean or some other such highbrow insult. You will know that you have really succeeded with your guests if they pat their stomach and turn purple while trying to suppress a belch. Just be ready with a "Hindlick Maneuver" in case that belch turns out to be more than simply a little gas.

Spaghetti

Serving Size: 6
Preparation Time: 20 minutes
Ingredients:
1 pound spaghetti
1 jar or can of your favorite marinara sauce
1 onion—diced
1 pound hamburger
4 fresh mushrooms—sliced
3 cloves garlic—crushed or cut up very small
1 dash black pepper
1 dash red pepper

Get your biggest pot on the stove. Pour in a gallon or so of water. Set it on your highest heat setting. The object here is to create superheated steam—or at least boiling water.

While you are waiting for the big pot to heat up, get out a saucepan and toss in the burger. Brown the burger and add onions, mushrooms and garlic. You may strain off the fat. If it is a fairly lean burger, it will be mostly broth and you can drink it just to horrify your wife (she will think you are slurping up solid oil). If it is a lean burger, you can also leave the broth in the sauce to good effect.

When the burger has browned, add the remaining ingredients to the sauce (except the spaghetti). Stir and keep warm on simmer until the spaghetti noodles are cooked.

Now cook noodles in pot per package.

Strain noodles, flop on plates, spoon on sauce. Serve hot.

Serving Suggestion: Good with garlic bread, never with corn.

Suggested Beer: Home brew with sediment.

Lasagna

Serving Size: 10
Preparation Time: 30 minutes
Ingredients:
1 box lasagna noodles
1½ pounds hamburger
16 ounces ricotta cheese
8 ounces mozzarella cheese—grated
¼ cup Parmesan cheese
1 can or jar marinara sauce
1 onion—diced
4 cloves garlic—chopped up very small
4 sliced fresh mushrooms
2 eggs
1 tablespoon parsley
1 dash pepper
1 dash basil

In a large pot, set water to boil.

Meanwhile, brown burger, onion, mushrooms and garlic. Add marinara and set aside.

Mix cheeses and eggs in a separate bowl with parsley and spices. Save back about one quarter of the mozzarella for the top.

When water in pot is boiling, add the lasagna noodles. You typically do not need to wait until the noodles are edible because they will be cooked in the oven as well. When noodles are ready (8 minutes or so) begin layering the various mixtures in a 9×13-inch pan. Start with the burger mixture; add the cheese, then the noodles. Keep layering until you run out of ingredients. Add the reserved mozzarella last.

Cover dish with foil and pop into oven at 375° for an hour or so. If you want to harden off the top, pull off the foil for the last 15 minutes.

DESSERTS

Real men don't make desserts. However, we will eat them on special occasions.

INDEX

T

V

Z

Printed in the United States
19147LVS00001B/94